Marriage and the Memo Method

MARRIAGE
AND THE
MEMO METHOD

by
PAUL A. HAUCK
and
EDMUND S. KEAN

THE WESTMINSTER PRESS

Philadelphia

BOOK DESIGN BY DOROTHY ALDEN SMITH

Published by The Westminster Press ®
Philadelphia, Pennsylvania

PRINTED IN THE UNITED STATES OF AMERICA

Library of Congress Cataloging in Publication Data

Hauck, Paul A
  Marriage and the memo method.

  Bibliography: p.
  1. Communication in marriage.   2. Memorandums.
3. Rational-emotive psychotherapy.   I. Kean,
Edmund S., 1915–   joint author.   II. Title.
HQ734.H383   301.42′7   75–23291
ISBN 0–664–24781–4

CONTENTS

PREFACE

The most difficult relationship in the whole world is not between you and your boss, between one nation and another, or between you and your neighbor. It is between you and your spouse. Nothing is so filled with tension or bliss as the marriage relationship. This is so, precisely because marriages have a unique ability to be the best and the worst experience of mankind. Learning how to have a happy marriage is well worth all the effort you can possibly devote to it.

Among the numerous pitfalls that can injure a happy relationship is poor communication. If you do not know what your spouse is talking about, you are not going to understand what problems you face. Nor will you know how to deal with them. It is, therefore, extremely important for you to learn how to communicate your frustrations to your mate and for your mate to communicate his or her frustrations to you. This is an extremely difficult thing to do.

Although we all speak our native tongue—and with reasonable clarity, so that everybody else understands us—it is simply a fact that the most difficult communication in the world is between husband and wife.

It is not a rarity to find persons who insist that they

have been saying something to their spouse for twenty years and yet their mate has never seemed to comprehend the message. For example, one man told his wife that if she did not stop nagging, he would divorce her. He warned her for years and finally did it. She, in turn, was shocked that he would do such a thing. When it was pointed out to her that he had threatened to leave her many times, she simply retorted: "Oh, of course I heard him threaten divorce, but I never believed it. How was I to know the fool really meant what he said?"

This is the crux of the matter. To have a happy relationship, a primary ingredient is the ability to communicate. This book is written to help in that vital process.

It could be assumed that after so many thousands of years of trial and error the institution of marriage must have reached its peak. With all the experience the race has had, it should know how to find pure bliss by now. Far from it! Contrary to all logic, the situation has worsened. Philandering husbands (even old Abraham made a pass at his maid) or oversexed wives, tired of their nagging husbands (remember beautiful Helena), give marriage a rather poor reputation.

As far back as history records, the male was dominant in the marriage partnership. He hunted, fought battles, worked at two jobs, and paid the mortgage. For these backbreaking activities, he had the honor of presiding at the family table and directing the family's affairs.

Woman complied, more or less willingly, accepting her station as second in command. By using her wit and wiles with cunning she often became the power behind the throne. Marriage in this fashion survived, at least statistically.

When civilized nations finally accepted the political and economic equality of women, the road toward meaningful and understanding cooperation in marriage was opened. It should have led to an easy clarification of many unsolved marital problems. The contrary happened! Liberated from antiquated ideas, woman pushed onward, often replacing the dominant man and putting her own individual stamp on daily life. In a direct assault on the old-fashioned ideas of her parents, she often expressed her own desires, chose her own partner at will, and expressed her sexuality as men have always done. Not surprisingly, this attack on ancient social and moral standards created resentment among men from mild tolerance to outright hostility. Soon, marriages based on this new concept of equality floundered by the thousands. Two forces were now set on a collision course. The ensuing clash of egos completely disrupted communication lines that were already frayed. Admittedly, many married couples found their own compromises and continued to "live happily ever after." On the whole, however, the divorce rate rose alarmingly and is still climbing.

Essentially for this reason we have engaged in the task of devising a new method to facilitate communication within marriage. Not that improving communication is going to solve all the problems a couple may encounter. That would be beautiful, if possible, but marriage is far too complex to be handled that neatly.

The chances, however, for a marriage to survive will obviously increase when ways are found for constructive criticism to be expressed in a calm atmosphere for the sake of mutual understanding.

We feel we have a sound method that can help any marriage to some extent. If you are having problems with your partner (at one time or another this includes everyone who is married), we believe you can be helped. Some persons will be helped enormously; others only a little. The principles set forth in this book have helped many to reduce their marital conflicts to manageable dimensions. We believe you too will find help if you study our methods carefully, put them into practice frequently, and go back to the text as often as necessary for guidance.

P. A. H. and E. S. K.

1

A NEW WAY
TO COMMUNICATE

The increasing number of broken marriages calls for effective steps to counter this tendency. A great many books have been written on this subject, offering explanations and advice. Many readers have sought help from these books but have had difficulty in translating their content into everyday practice. Lectures and adult evening courses that tried to round out information to newlyweds and give counsel to the divorce-minded were more successful because of the dialogue they provoked. Trained counselors in private and group sessions have made every effort to iron out marital difficulties. However, an insufficient number of counselors and the high expense involved have restricted this approach to only a few of the vast number who need help.

While, initially, most divorces occurred within the younger age groups, soon older couples in increasing numbers sought dissolution of their marital ties. Under the impact of prolonged misunderstandings and lack of communication, even marriages that appeared stable began to crumble. It became obvious that an easier, less costly way had to be found for husband and wife to air their complaints. This book is offered as a fresh approach to help fill this need.

The dictionary defines communication as "the act of imparting ideas to someone else." The most common means of communication is by words, written or spoken. Unfortunately, nature has not endowed all persons with equal skills to express themselves, thus many thoughts remain unspoken and many spoken words are misunderstood.

Our experience over long years of working with couples who come to us for advice reveals that the most common blocks to intimate discussions are emotional ones. An involuntary sneer, a raised voice, a contemptuous look, or a stream of tears often abruptly terminates serious efforts to talk about a significant problem. An attempt to express a reasonable grievance or to make a timely suggestion was misinterpreted. Suddenly the atmosphere turns hostile and the scene ends in tears and slammed doors. Vanity and hurt pride take the place of understanding and are the catalyst of irreparable quarrels.

Listening to the end results of too many such marital skirmishes, we came upon a way to avoid them altogether. Instead of perpetuating futile arguments, why not simply state in writing the problem at issue? Thus the "Memo Method" was born. Notes made about grievances in the absence of the partner will attain greater objectivity than an emotional face-to-face confrontation possibly can. The object of the Memo Method is to make husbands and wives think before they write down a suggestion or complaint.

Nothing is more patient than paper. Written and read in solitude, without interference of personalities, the problem is stated much more objectively and less irritably. Once a sound basis for communication is established, a couple may carry on peacefully for a long time.

The question remains, How can this state be achieved?

We have found that written communication is frequently so distinctive an act that it catches a person unaware and makes him or her realize that something important is being said.

The written word has the same effect as a mother beckoning her child—"Jimmy Jones, you get into the house!" We all recognize that by using his first and last names she means business and he is about to be told something rather serious. The same tactic is applied in a written message to or from your mate. Something may have been said to you over the phone or across the dinner table a number of times, but the full impact is not nearly as strong as a written message, because writing represents a very earnest attempt to say precisely what you want to say.

Let us first attempt to describe how the method works. We will then suggest the reasons why writing rather than just talking or why actions instead of complaining are more effective techniques. We will also explore the reasons why persons shy away from forcefully communicating in their writing and their behavior.

HOW THE MEMO METHOD WORKS

The next time you are frustrated by your mate, take a separate sheet of paper and write the word PROBLEM in the upper left-hand corner. Then, in as clear and concise a manner as possible, state the problem. Try to limit it to one or two sentences.

"I cannot stand your drinking anymore," or "You never back me up when it comes to disciplining the children," or "You are always correcting me and I'm supposed to take that calmly, but if I correct you once, you become very defensive." These are examples of typical problems.

Once the problem has been stated, start another paragraph and write the word CAUSES in the left-hand margin. Under the heading CAUSES list all the reasons why you think your mate acts in the way that disturbs you. For example, some responses you may list for the last problem mentioned above ("You are always correcting me and I'm supposed to take that calmly, but if I correct you once, you become very defensive") might be:

1. "You are overly sensitive and think you have to be perfect. For that reason, when I criticize you in a normal way, you cannot stand it."

2. "Your parents have always criticized you, and when I do, you think I'm putting you down just like they did."

3. "You've had a couple of failures in your life recently and I think you have become very touchy over them. As a result, you have become needlessly sensitive about having *anybody* find fault with you."

After CAUSES comes the most important step of all—the proposed SOLUTIONS. Write the word SOLUTIONS in the left-hand margin and again list the possibilities that you feel will clear up the problem. In this case, we might suggest the following:

1. "Stop and realize, honey, you are a worthwhile being even if you have your failures."

2. "I hope you don't mind if I remind you when you get in this mood that I am not your mother (or your father). I am your wife (or husband) and love you very much. Let me suggest a good book you can read that will show you what a worthwhile person you are, although you have some faults. Maybe some of our friends know of a good book that will help us in this matter."

3. "If this problem persists, I would recommend that you seek professional counseling. In the final analysis, it is nothing less than an inferiority complex and I am sure it can be helped. Even when you think I am wrong to criticize you, try to remind yourself that I have a right to be mistaken. Everyone has a right to be wrong. I do not feel I am mistaken by making these comments, so grant me the right to my opinion although it is different from your opinion."

The plaintiff could go on proposing possible solutions until the subject is thoroughly covered.

Next, the defendant is encouraged to take a sheet of paper and make the same sort of analysis the plaintiff has made. The defendant should write out the problem as he or she sees it, and write out causes and solutions in an identical manner, but from his or her point of view.

After studying each other's papers, both should sit down over a cup of coffee when the mood is particularly calm and discuss what each has written. In most cases the discussion will proceed in a rational and open manner and the issue can be managed.

If satisfaction is not derived from the post-memo session, then each can write an additional memo concerning the new matters brought to light during the conference.

And so it can go on for years and years with numerous memos passing back and forth, each partner calmly presenting and defending and perhaps modifying his or her case. These memos can be kept as a running diary of tribulations and growth in the family experience. At some future time the couple can sit back and review their memos and realize that although their marriage had its ups and downs, they overcame significant difficulties which at one time terribly concerned them.

In Chapter 6 you will note further examples of the Memo Method used in a significant number of vital areas of married life. These examples are meant only as guidelines to help you get acquainted with the Memo Method and to show how you can apply it to whatever problems may arise in your own marriage.

There are, of course, as many problems in marriage as there are married couples, but the principle of the Memo Method can be applied to all.

It is our hope·that this book will help you to become a psychologically sound person and to understand the complex dynamics within marriage itself. When you are armed with that knowledge and the ability to communicate with your mate, the chances of improving your love life with your mate should definitely increase.

We have attempted to deal with the most common marital controversies. These include: Love in Marriage; Sexuality in Marriage; Entertainment, Sports, Hobbies, and Vacations; The Rearing of Children; Finances; Relatives and Friends; Religion, Politics, and Philosophy of Life.

Keep the memos you write as documentation of your marital experience. They can be read again and again as guidelines for a happy marriage. The true nature of the relationship between a husband and wife can be revealed through an examination of the prolonged accumulation of notes. If professional counseling is necessary, the memos can be of great value to the counselor for obtaining a better inside knowledge of the marital problems of a couple.

HOW TO COMMUNICATE AND WHEN

The key to ventilating one's ideas, convincing another person, or reaching a compromise is communication by dialogue. The bridge to mutual understanding is built with words (spoken or written), nonverbal signs, and actions. Whatever the means, there must be communication in order to attain understanding. Marriage is the ideal relationship for practicing the skills of communicating.

The easiest way to communicate is by spoken word. Anyone possessing a language can say what is on his mind. There is no need to be a poet or an orator to do this. The simplest sentence can often say more than a flowery speech.

Yet it has been established that many persons are more willing to write down their thoughts than to talk. A word once spoken cannot be retrieved and is often misunderstood. Also, words are cheap. A fast talker can overwhelm with a flood of verbiage. A fluent talker is able to bowl over initial resistance from a hesitant listener and achieve his goal by persuasion.

Remember how the high-pressure salesman can outtalk a customer in such a convincing manner that many of us have been stuck with unwanted goods at one time or another? Equally convincing is the roaming lover who has been caught but knows how to talk himself out of his predicament with soft words and by denying any wrongdoing.

Words can be twisted, forgotten, and denied. Has it not happened to you? You repeatedly mention a certain wish or complaint and your partner indignantly insists that he or she never heard it. When we don't want to listen, we easily forget ever conversing about the subject. This is particularly so if the subject is an unpleasant one.

In politics, words have been misused so often that a campaign promise is seldom taken seriously by the public. Quotes are called misquotes; remarks are ascribed to poor reporting. Who is to know the truth? My word against yours is a stalemate.

We have reached the point where only the written and signed contract is valid. Long gone are the days when a word and a handshake sealed a deal.

Words are not always misused for some ulterior, dark purpose. I recall the woman who loved her husband dearly but could not prevent her tongue from prattling along whenever they were with company. She would belittle her husband in a benign and teasing manner.

He never objected in public, but when they returned home, he rebuked her for her remarks. Invariably she denied having said the things he referred to or she passed them off as jokes. She knew how to make him forget her remarks, and in the end he was not sure himself whether he had heard correctly. One day, at a party, he decided to prove his case. Secretly he equipped himself with a small tape recorder and made a record of everything she said.

After the party, faced with the undeniable evidence,

she realized what she had been doing and promised to change.

Another case involved a husband whose habit was to drop his shoes, socks, and underwear all over the house when he came home from work. Repeated reprimands from his wife were of no avail. One day she collected all his dirty clothes and deposited them on his worktable with an appropriate note attached.

Faced with the memo and the heap of dirty laundry, he realized how his carelessness had offended her and he thereafter ceased the old practice.

Words alone, even spoken or written clearly, do not necessarily communicate. They must be heard and understood. Also there must be a willingness from both mates to respond to what is expressed.

"When is the best time to communicate?" Anytime! Whenever you feel that communication is needed. The more quickly you react to a problem, the better, provided the circumstances are appropriate. It is not wise, for example, to air your private differences in the presence of others. But do not put off facing a problem that needs attention. Nothing threatens the fabric of a marriage more deeply than grudges and suppressed resentments. Therefore, if something is bothering you, get it out of your system—communicate!

TALK IS CHEAP

Isn't it surprising that one of the most difficult things for a married couple to do is to communicate their honest feelings to each other? This seems odd indeed, since most people have adequate verbal skills. They can read. They have written hundreds of letters. They easily engage in daily conversations with their neigh-bors, salesclerks, and family members. Still, it is an easily verified observation that talk is often a poor way to get a message across to anyone. Why? Because either we do not listen very carefully or we simply do not believe what we're told.

Let us cite some examples. A couple came to us for counseling because the husband was leaning more and more upon his wife, and not listening to her protests. He was merrily going on his way as though she had never uttered a word to him.

He was a hard-driving salesman. He had learned long ago that the secret to success in selling was simply to ignore a customer's protests. He plowed ahead, often making sales where the more timid salesmen would have backed off. This technique worked perfectly well at selling, but it was murder when it came to his mar-riage.

After they had a few counseling sessions, it was quite obvious that the wife had to do something other than just talk to her husband. She was encouraged to try something different to express her feelings. We sug-gested she write or take some other calculated action—most of all, discontinue simply saying things to him when he refused to listen.

Her major complaint was that he fell asleep in the middle of the evening while he was watching televi-sion. She wanted his company because she had no op-portunity to talk to anyone all day long. She told him again and again how frustrated his falling asleep made her. One would have thought he would have listened sooner or later. He never did!

Finally, one evening when he dozed off she went into the kitchen, filled a pitcher with water, returned to the living room and slowly poured the water on his head. When the last drop hit his nose, she said, "Get the message?" That was the last time he went to sleep early in the evening.

We don't recommend this method if you have an aggressive husband, or do not carry Blue Shield. But in this case it was effective.

In another instance, a wife wanted very much to talk to her husband before he went on the road on Monday morning. He insisted he had to move along because he was late. Whatever they had to talk about could wait, he said. She urged him to stay, because there were a number of matters she still had to discuss with him. Waiting four days for his return would be too frustrating. Another half hour couldn't ruin his business, she emphasized. She further pointed out that he was always running off whenever she had something important to tell him. Nevertheless, the fellow took off in his car.

After he left, the wife went into the room that served as her husband's office in the home, picked up the stack of orders he had written up the week before, retyped each one and put them aside in a drawer. She then systematically ripped up each one and left the heap of shreds on the desk with a note describing why she did this and how she felt about it.

Needless to say, her husband got the message!

We could go on and on giving illustrations about how people listen much better when something other then ordinary talk becomes the means of communication. Writing notes or letters falls in the same category as pouring water on someone's head or tearing up a salesman's orders. It is an act or form of behavior that says something quite irrefutable. Talk can often be disregarded, but a note cannot so easily be ignored. When you write a message, your mate has to look it over and think about it. A reply requires study and reflection, a leisurely consideration of what an appropriate response requires.

Some people listen through their eyes rather than through their ears. When this is the case, the marriage memo is an ideal method for getting a message across. Do not underestimate the power of the pen. A few words put on paper are worth a thousand words yelled by you and your mate at each other in the middle of the night.

FEAR OF THE TRUTH

Fear is another major block to communication between two people. First, you fear that the other person will be upset by what you have to say. Secondly, you fear being rejected for telling the truth. And thirdly, you believe you could not stand that rejection because you *must* have the other person's love.

Let us look at the first fear. No matter what you have to say to your mate, you cannot upset him or her by it. People do not upset others emotionally, they can upset others only physically. That's right!

When your mate is angry or weepy over something you have said or done, never blame yourself for his or her emotional disturbance. Our mates disturb themselves by what they said to *themselves* in response to what we did or said.

For example, suppose you told your husband you thought his mother was an old busybody. Let us further suppose he became quite incensed over the remark. You might feel guilty because you would think, "I am the one who made him so upset." Stop thinking this way! It simply is not true. You are not the one who upset him in this case. Rather, he upsets himself by telling himself you have no right to think his mother is a busybody.

Do not let reactions on the part of other people control your life. Say what you have to say, and if your words are not understood, write them down on a memo as honestly and as politely as you can. But get it said! Whatever emotional reaction the other person has is *his* problem, not yours. If he cannot stand the truth, then tell him to go to a counselor and find out how he can remain undisturbed over unpleasant pieces of news. Even if he goes into depression and is hospitalized, he is still upsetting himself completely.

To understand this, you must understand the distinction between a frustration and a disturbance. It is quite true that upon relaying bad news or something harsh to our mates, we are indeed frustrating them. No one wants to hear unpleasant things and this is a frustration of the most common sort.

However, do *not* assume that simply because you have frustrated your mate you have also disturbed him. Frustrating him has been your end of the behavior pattern, but his disturbing himself (over your frustrations) is his end of the behavior pattern. He has control over what he does about your frustrations and if he will talk to himself more sensibly and rationally, he will certainly not upset himself. In other words, he has the choice of whether he will react to frustration calmly or neurotically. If he tells himself, "It's terrible that she thinks this way about my mother," or "It's awful that she wants to leave and is unhappy in this marriage," then he is bound to be upset. If, on the other hand, he says to himself, "She has every right to her views, perhaps I have been wrong about some of her beliefs," he will not be disturbed.

To appreciate this concept, it is necessary to understand the ABC's of emotions. If someone throws a dagger at you (let's call the dagger A) and it gives you a pain in your chest (let's call the pain C), it is safe to say that A causes C in reference to physical pain.

Now let's suppose that instead of a knife your spouse throws several cutting words at you such as "dummy" or "stupid." Let's call those cutting words A. You are likely to feel upset and hurt at C (your body). Again you are going to insist that A, the harsh words, caused C, the hurt. *Not so!* The emotional pain is never caused by what your mate says or does unless it can affect you physically in a direct way. Since words cannot cut the skin or break bones, they are not the direct causes of your pain. Then what is the cause of your pain? It is B, the irrational thoughts you have about A. Your *thinking* upsets and hurts you, not what is said to you by someone else.

The probable irrational thoughts in the above example were: (1) "It's awful and terrible if I don't get what I want." This is irrational because it cannot be demonstrated that he *has* to have everything he wants, or that not getting what he wants *is awful.* (2) "You should be blamed for saying unkind remarks about my mother." Why should anyone be severely blamed for saying unkind things of someone else? Don't we have the right to our opinions? How can words hurt anyone?

This analysis could go much farther. It is based on the theory of rational-emotive therapy (RET). Those who wish to study the subject more fully will find a recommended reading list at the end of this book.

The second major reason for not communicating our honest feelings to our mates is that we are afraid of being rejected by them. Thus we do not want to bring up touchy issues. This fear is based on the false assumption that we *have* to have people's approval and are *no good* unless we have it. Therefore, to avoid rejection we must suffer in silence.

Unless you learn to challenge the whole idea that you have to have your mate's affection all the time, you're in for trouble. It would be perfectly delightful if that were possible. Such love is impossible, but we act as though we were going to die when we sense that our mate is angry with us and is about to reject us.

What is so awful about being rejected at times? How can it really hurt? When you examine this matter carefully you will see that rejection is painless. Annoying, yes; sad, yes; but catastrophic, no! If you are in a continuous state of rejection, you really don't have a marriage. But even that is not the end of the world any more than it would be the end of the world if your mate died. He or she could not love you then and you would simply have to bolster your courage and get along in life without your loved one. Therefore, it is sheer nonsense to insist that you should be mightily upset because you are not particularly well liked by your mate for a short period of time.

Fear of rejection is just about the strongest fear that plagues us and it is the most common fear as well. It is not the fear of strangers, fear of injury, fear of cancer, or anything else as much as the fear of rejection that makes cowards of us. We will not do what we feel deep in our heart we should do, simply because we think we must be loved by some important other person and that speaking the truth will destroy that love. Again, we do not need it. It is only wonderful to have it in the same way that it is nice to have mushrooms on steak, and it is not even necessary to have steak. One can always eat grains.

In the same way it is delightful to have the love of one's family, parents, and spouse constantly, but it certainly is not necessary. You are not going to go up in smoke because someone hates you for three days. Go about your business for a while, stand pat, and let time take care of the other person's emotional reaction toward whatever you had to say.

So, use these marriage memos as a means of expressing your deepest feelings. Stop being a coward about what you feel. If speaking up does not do the trick, then get out your pencil or your ballpoint pen and write down what you are feeling. Don't be sheepish or timid; spell it out in big, bold letters so there is no confusing the message.

Remember always, you are not responsible for any disturbance he or she may have as a result of your message. And if you get rejected in the process, so what? It won't kill you. Instead, we can practically guarantee that the benefits you will receive from this open and honest communication will far outweigh the temporary inconvenience you may suffer because you were rejected.

2

ACHIEVING EQUALITY
IN MARRIAGE

The Memo Method of communicating is quite pointless unless we can feel comfortable about expressing our grievances. If you are afraid to stand up for your rights, then even the finest methods for communicating your concerns will do you no good. Suppose you feel terribly guilty about wanting something that could improve your marriage but will inconvenience your mate. If you fail to express how you feel, no method can help you.

To help you communicate effectively, you must first develop a feeling of being your mate's equal. Not superior or subordinate, but equal! To do this, you will have to learn to detect emotional blackmail and how to spot strategies used by your mate to get you to give up your desire for change.

STRATEGIES OF EMOTIONAL BLACKMAIL

Change in a relationship is always uncomfortable for a person who is asked to do the changing. You can almost always expect some resistance against doing things a new way. Sometimes that resistance can become fantastically stubborn. Sometimes what you are asking of your mate may seem so threatening that there is simply no way to go along with it. The response is then to figure out some means to get you to abandon your request. What often happens in such cases is that your mate will have a plan, a strategy, or a game to convince you to give up. If that plan doesn't work, don't be lulled into a false sense of security. You have only weathered the first storm. Strategy number two is just over the horizon. After you have stuck to your guns, you must still be patient, because your mate may be coming along with strategy number three.

There is no limit to the number of ploys you will face until your mate is completely convinced you mean what you say and are not about to budge. At that point you will have won the war, because you would have won all the battles. The important point, however, is that you must see through your mate's behavior during this time. The series of plans you confront are not devised as a response to what you ask. Rather, they are offered in the hope that they will be scary enough, threatening enough, guilt-provoking enough, to get you to back down.

Let's look at the case of a typical series of strategies. A wife wants more freedom to go to school, to go out bowling with her girl friends on a Friday night, to have her own checking account, or to use one of the two family cars. Her husband is mightily threatened by this demand for independence, although he has had all these liberties since they were married. He really isn't confident that he can keep his wife unless he has her under control. Therefore, he can't accept a state of equality. How will he respond? He is going to try to convince her to give up these requests, to stay home like a good girl, and to mind the home fires while he goes out and has a carefree time as he has always done.

Put yourself in his place. What would you do about the situation in order to get your wife to stay home?

Your first move might be to get angry with her. If in the past she has been sensitive and touchy to yelling, why not try this technique again? Give her a good bawling out, scream awhile, throw a few things, threaten her with your fist and see if she doesn't back away. You might even try manhandling her a bit. This is usually fear-provoking and might even cause the kids to get a little panicky, thereby surely bringing her to her senses.

But behold, the wife still insists upon doing the same things you've always done. So what do you do now? Employ strategy number two! This time you try to make her feel guilty. You point out how hard you are working and, therefore, what's so bad about having some free time in the evening up at the tavern with a few of the boys! A man has to relax and unwind a bit, doesn't he? Hasn't he been a decent fellow and given her a nice home? Does he run around like some men? No. He's a decent guy who cares for his family and all he wants is their happiness. How can she do this to someone who cares so much for her? She's ungrateful and she has hurt him deeply (sniff, sniff). Can't she see what she is doing to him?

This is a powerful strategy, practically guaranteed to bring a strong woman to her knees. If our subject knows what is happening, she will recognize the strategy he is using to get her to change her mind and she will stand pat. Otherwise he will be running her life again and she will be right back where she started.

Anger and guilt have not worked, so now he has to use strategy number three: threat of desertion. He'll leave her and the kids because she has made life intolerable. Why should he be around to burden her if he is such a crummy guy? She'll be better off without him anyway. He can't live in a situation that is so painful to him. He might as well get out and let her have it her own way.

"Where is my bag, honey?" Never mind, he won't go. It's only another escalated threat to make her back down.

This is emotional blackmail. It is saying: "Unless you give me what I want, I will see to it that your soul roasts in hell for eternity. I don't care how you feel or how much you suffer. I will get even with you because you are frustrating me!"

These are not the words of a lover. They are the words of a totally selfish and immature person who wants his own happiness at the price of others' misery.

Fortunately we have a way out of this dilemma. If you are being emotionally blackmailed, simply stop and realize that *you are permitting it.* Nobody can blackmail you unless you allow it. You never need to feel guilty because of another person's threats or because somebody blames you for making him or her agitated. This is something the other person is doing to himself, you are not doing it to him. If he wants to do some drastic thing over some behavior of yours, tell him to go right ahead. But also tell the person you are sorry and it would be a big loss to you.

Emotional blackmail usually stops quickly when the person realizes that you are not going to get shook up over his or her emotional disturbances.

If you do give in to emotional blackmail, you are going to encourage that person to use more emotional blackmail against you. Once a strategy like this works, it tends to be used again and again. Therefore, if you really want to save someone from going to extremes, don't let the threat become effective. That is, don't make it a rewarding experience for the other person. This means that you must allow the person to be mildly frustrated after making the threats. He or she will then see that using that strategy simply does not work. You will have to wait and see what happens next.

If the first three strategies have not worked, we can expect our irate gentleman to come up with a fourth. He may threaten to go out with other women. He may deliberately stay out late, lie about having an affair, be cold sexually, and in any number of ways give the impression that he is disinterested in you totally. Whatever he does, the show is supposed to be impressive and convincing. If you sit tight and do not let this tactic sway you, you may be well rewarded. Eventually the point will be reached where he will actually sever the relationship or listen to your case and come to terms with your demands. In most cases it will likely be the latter.

We hope the point is made that when you threaten your mate with plans for change, you must expect a time of turmoil in the manner just described above. It is the rare partner who takes a demand for change with calmness and rationality.

Therefore, when you sit down to communicate in writing what you think causes your unhappiness and what solutions you think might help to resolve the problems, do so forthrightly, knowing full well that you are about to go into a stressful period of interaction. So be it! The sooner these issues are faced, the sooner the battle will be over. Knowing what some of the reactions might be, you are much better prepared for the coming neurotic reactions of your spouse.

RISK-TAKING IN MARRIAGE

When two persons marry, they almost invariably come from different backgrounds. This is more the case today than it has ever been. This means that one person's tastes are often vastly different from another's. For instance, one person knows how to swim, the other does not. One may enjoy chess and the other likes poker. One enjoys the seashore but the other prefers the mountains. One enjoys dancing and the other is happy just listening to music.

It is a common observation that those marriages which are the soundest are also those in which both partners engage in similar activities fairly frequently. It is so much more satisfying to go to a bridge game with your mate than with a stranger. Looking at a painting with someone who also appreciates that kind of beauty is more rewarding than seeing it alone. Listening to a classical record or a jazz quintet is so much more enjoyable if your mate is as enraptured with that style of music as you are. In short, the more you have in common as far as tastes and recreations go, the better.

How do you develop these common interests if you do not have them already? Simply by forcing yourself into these activities, staying with them with an open mind, and sometimes risking even your safety to overcome your fears so that you can share some interests with your mate. For example, one woman who complained about her husband's refusal to water-ski, found life a great deal more enjoyable when, after counseling, he was urged to try water-skiing no matter how fearful he was of it. He was a reasonably good swimmer, but somehow the fear of getting himself tied up in the propeller blades or taking a bad spill and breaking a bone out in the middle of the lake held him back. He was urged to compare the odds of that happening with the likelihood of being injured in a car, an airplane, or an elevator. There, too, freak accidents happen, but he seldom gave them a second thought. Finally he was persuaded to get on water skis. He tried it several times and actually began to enjoy it. In fact, he became so skilled that he and his wife became a team of water skiers who gave exhibitions for the local community.

The same can happen with dancing, bridge-playing, cooking gourmet meals, and so on. Although you may not be very good at these activities at first, if they are important to your mate, stick with them. Do not keep telling yourself how awful and terrible they are. Rather, keep an open mind and continually remind yourself that a lot of things you once were afraid of or disliked, you have since learned to tolerate or even to enjoy. If you realize that it makes someone else happy, keep your grudges to yourself. Take a chance. Put yourself out a bit, and if need be, risk your safety from time to time if it is a step in the direction of making the marriage better.

This does not mean that you have to join the sky divers club simply because your husband is nuts about the sport. However, if you could force yourself to do even that, you might find again that you enjoy it enormously and also overcome your fear in due course, as most sky divers have apparently been able to do. Fortunately, however, it is not these kinds of physically dangerous situations that most of us fear. More commonly it is having certain people over for a visit. Or it is standing up for your opinion in company. Or it is simply talking up to your mate. Take the risk, communicate your dislikes and your disapproval. But do not let fear run your life. Say what you have to, and both of you will be happier for it eventually. At first the relationship will be strained, but that cannot be helped. You cannot make an omelet without cracking eggs, as they say. And no marriage can get its problems aired if no one has the courage to raise them.

TYPICAL ISSUES THAT REQUIRE TAKING RISKS

For the sake of illustration, let us refer to several risk-taking issues that involve the woman only. In this day of the liberated woman we find that she can really stand up against her husband if she wants to go to work. This is not a problem with most husbands. But for the husband who is unsure of the hold he has on his wife, this move can be devastating. He may find himself getting jealous and threatened by the possibility of her meeting any number of good-looking and virile men. He becomes very upset over the thought of her leaving the home, where he knows she is safe from such entice-ments. To stand up against the emotional attack that he most likely will launch, she should be prepared for the worst. A jealous man is going to come on with one tactic after another in an attempt to keep her home, where, in his opinion, she belongs.

If she allows herself to be threatened to stay at home, she will have set a pattern for the rest of her married life. If she permits him to make her feel guilty, she will set a precedent that will be used by him for years to come. If he threatens to step out on her, cut her funds off, not let her have the use of the car, she should try to meet each of these objections as forcefully as possible. She can call a cab. She can threaten divorce if he will not fund her properly. She could show him in no uncertain way that she has no intention of knuckling under to his threats. Instead of giving in to him, she might make him understand that he has a problem and ought to go see a psychotherapist.

When a woman gets into situations where she might meet men, jealous husbands always seem to have a very bad time of it. In this day and age, women are not hesitant to spend some time as they wish without their husbands in the company of other women. This is again one of those times when a wife will have to risk all the husband's wrath and simply go about her business in the social way that she wants to. As long as she knows that she is conducting herself properly, there is no reason in the world why she should not go and enjoy herself occasionally. If he makes himself miserable over what she is doing, she ought not to feel guilty in the slightest but ought to recognize that he has failed to take care of his own neurosis. If he enjoys being miserable, let him be miserable. If he desires to rid himself of unwarranted jealousy, the wife could encourage him to seek counsel and have this matter straightened out. The responsibility for his misery and his upsets are solely his, not hers.

The same might be said if the wife returns again to school. This is one of those threatening situations where she might fall in love with another man and this may be more than the jealous husband can take. He may threaten not to give her funds, to bother her during her studies, and to do all kinds of devious things in order to get her to give up her plans. However, the wise wife does not accept such threats. She simply takes the risk and sticks to her guns, because she knows that there is nothing inherently wrong in what she is doing. School is an admirable goal and there is no reason in the world why she should not educate herself further if that pleases her. And if he cannot stand it, then let him take to the therapeutic couch.

Let us now consider the husband as the plaintiff in these illustrations. What is he likely to do? He may repeatedly insist that it is his wife's responsibility to make him happy and to desist from doing what creates his unhappiness. He has concluded that happiness will come to him once again when she straightens out her crazy thinking, behaves like a sane woman, and stays home like a good housewife. He literally believes this. But do not be deceived, you who are mates of such insecure people. The truth is that you do not have to turn yourself inside out to make the other person happy. Happiness has only partially to do with how you behave. People who are *demanding* that you behave the way they want you to are simply spoiled and inconsiderate. They are turning their anger on because they are not getting their way.

When this happens it is imperative that you see the justice in your own role, that you do not assume responsibility for the other person's miseries. Psychological studies of anger show that many of us become angry because we are childishly *insisting* upon getting what we want. When your husband turns red with fury because you are not about to do what he insists you must do, he is acting the role of a spoiled little boy who isn't getting his lollipop.

Do not give him everything he wants or you will condition him to be more spoiled than he was before. Every time you yield to his neurotic demands he becomes more of a tyrant. If you really want equality in marriage, help him to become a more mature person, one whom you can live with for the rest of your married life. Do not give him everything he wants under the disguise that you love him. Love is not pampering. Rather, it seeks to encourage the best that is possible in another. It is a misunderstanding to think that we only express love when we are doing what the other person wants. Neurotic people often demand things that really aren't good for them. You would surely not give your own child an endless diet of ice cream or candy simply because you love the child. In fact, you would see such behavior as anything but love. The same applies to your mate. Do not indulge your mate in every request or you will simply spoil him to a point where he becomes indignantly self-righteous and intolerably self-centered.

To get your mate to believe that your risk-taking is utterly serious, you must be prepared to show him what the consequences will be if he does not go along with some of your strong desires. He will, of course, make every conceivable attempt to get you to be the sweet nonentity you once were. To help him realize that those days are gone forever, you will need to identify what the bad effects will be if he does not agree to at least some of your desires. For example, if he insists upon making a scene in public, then tell him outright that you will simply call the police. Admittedly, he will be furious at you for this, but so be it. This is what we mean by taking risks. If you *allow* people to dominate you, then don't complain about it. But if you want ridiculous behavior stopped, then take the steps that are necessary to stop it.

Another area in which women sometimes have difficulty in taking the necessary risks is when they want to say "No" to an issue but are afraid of the immediate consequences. In other words, they want to keep the peace even though they really do not agree with what is happening. Your husband, for example, wants to go to one movie and you want to go to another. You are afraid he will say something unkind to you, so you give in. When you do that, you have not really done him a favor at all. When you realize that you have given in for the umpteenth time, you will begin to do a slow burn and eventually your husband will have to suffer from your unhappiness. It is impossible to be happy in a marriage if both partners are not truly happy. It is only a matter of time before there will be some conflict, some resentment, a fight, or threats of separation, if happiness is not mutual.

To have a happy marriage, you must take the risk and say "No" to your mate when you really mean it. Don't do him favors while underneath you feel disagreement and resentment. It is much more sensible at the beginning to say outright that you are against something. If there is to be a confrontation, have it at that time. Then he can at least have respect for your views, because you are not a phony. He has the right to accuse you of not telling the truth if you say that something is all right when you really don't mean it. That's nothing more nor less than telling a lie. He can't possibly know how to judge your behavior if you are repeatedly untruthful simply because you are afraid to express your opinion. It is much easier to face any disagreements that you might have right off than to have them a month later. It's better to learn sooner that you really didn't want to buy that house or to go west for a vacation than to accumulate disagreements later on.

All these problems entail some risk. This is especially

so when the mate is an unreasonable person. However, not to take such risks is even riskier. The amount of spoiling that goes on in our mates because we have avoided taking sensible risks is enormous. We only make our nest more miserable when we refuse to face unpleasant situations at the time they arise. To put off facing them, while feeling badly in the process, makes more serious trouble later. How much easier it is simply to face issues, have fights, and be over with the thing today than to settle for a false peace. To refuse to take the risk of confronting your mate means to suffer with the misery you got yourself into. Anytime this is worse than being honest—worse for yourself and for the other person as well.

The same might be said about a husband who beats his wife. She has every right to protect herself. If he becomes violent with her and it puts her in the hospital, she certainly ought not to allow it to happen a second time. She can let him know that she will either commit him to the state hospital or throw him into jail. She needn't worry about what the neighbors say, about what the newspapers print, or about her guilt. None of these reactions is sensible. You would not hesitate to throw an intruder who breaks into your home into jail. An assault remains what it is, a threat to your health, irrespective of who makes it. Determining your rights may seem coldhearted, but what basis is there for a marriage if basic human rights are not respected? If you do not demand this, you will be his slave for life.

Therefore, take your risks. You will be grateful for it and both of you will know where you stand. That's really what communication is all about. Understandably some mates are emotionally unable to face the truth head on. Their reactions may be violent or unreasonable and abort any further discussion. In such cases the Memo Method will help. It gives the mate time to digest what he or she was told and to react appropriately without blowing his or her cool.

CONTROLLING ANGER OVER FRUSTRATION

Anger is one of the big stumbling blocks in marriage. One of the most frequent emotional reactions that couples have is anger over money. This is a waste of time and accomplishes nothing. The angrier you get over the way your mate handles money, the more spiteful he or she may become in spending it. Besides, anger causes a great deal of distance between people and adds fuel to the fires of unrest. Instead of getting angry, communicate what you feel in direct terms, but spare yourself the misery of being furious. It is bad enough that your mate frustrates you sometimes in unfair ways. To compound this injustice by getting yourself upset is frequently the worst part of the entire situation. If your mate's extravagance amounts to X degrees of disturbance, then your anger over the extravagance multiplies it many more times. The resulting annoyance has increased considerably. That is just plain bad economics in both money and emotions.

Let us explore the psychology of anger. No one but you yourself makes you angry. It is what you say to yourself about the frustrations, not the frustrations themselves, that makes you upset. In this case, you are telling yourself that the other person is not giving you what you want, which is a fact, but that he or she *should* give you what you want, which is not a fact. There is no reason in the world why your mate *has* to be sensible with money or sensible in any other conceivable way. Just because you would *like* people to be sensible with you does not mean that they *have* to be that way. *People have a right to be wrong.* We are human beings and we are not necessarily bad when we behave badly. So stop getting angry when you are not getting your way.

In the final analysis, that is what most anger means. It means that you are having a minor temper tantrum. When you notice a child screaming and pounding his head on the floor because he does not get the candy he asked for, just think of yourself in the same terms. Whenever you get angry, you are doing precisely the same thing, except that you are doing it in an adult way. You usually don't stamp your foot and pound your head on the floor and cry like a baby. However, you are still acting like a baby by insisting that you *have* to have what you want. If you would stop insisting or making demands, you would banish a great deal of your anger. Imagine a marriage in which no one gets really angry. This is not to say that there should be no occasion to express oneself, even loudly. We are by no means advocating that couples become passive and let their mates walk over them. This is not healthy and it will not lead to a good marriage. We are only saying that in your attempt to stand up for yourself you do not have to act like a dictator. Whenever you are irrationally angry, you are acting like a dictator and a baby besides.

In addition, an angry person almost always wants to hurt the person who is doing the frustrating. This also causes enormous problems in marriage. Others do not improve their behavior because they are treated severely. Screaming at them, punishing them, and blaming them endlessly simply does not make them better people. Think of the last time you got a tongue-lashing. Did you feel refreshed and invigorated and healthy afterward? Of course you didn't. Why not? Simply because that kind of behavior leads to greater disturbance, not less. If that's the way verbal abuse affects you, why would others react differently? Children especially suffer from angry outbursts, just as we do. They have fewer defenses, fewer experiences to call upon in order to protect themselves against the harsh accusations that we parents sometimes make. So let us not be unreasonable with our children. The less angry we are with them while remaining firm, the better they are likely to turn out. The same is the case with our spouses. There are no bad people in the world, *there is only bad behavior.* So let us stop thinking that people are bad and can be improved by our being severe with them. This is nonsense and mythology from hundreds of years ago.

Obviously, being human, we often cannot control our anger. Therefore, the memo, so impersonal and calm, gives us a chance to express ourselves without provoking automatic and instant antagonism in the partner. Rather, it can start the chain reaction of rational and honest communication.

BLAME: THE MOST DANGEROUS PSYCHOLOGICAL ACT OF ALL

What really causes more marital unhappiness than anything else is blame. By this we mean making judgments about your mate on the basis of what he or she has done. Suppose your wife has failed to live up to her domestic obligations and this has disappointed you greatly. You would then be correct in assuming that she is a poor housekeeper, and if you stopped your criticisms at that point, you would be a healthy person. You would not be angry, and your wife might learn something from your rebuke. However, what most people do is to go one step farther. They conclude that not cleaning the house is a bad thing, and therefore the *mate is bad*. This interpretation confuses the person with the person's behavior. Whenever you attack what a person has done *and* the person himself, that is what we refer to as blame. So far as we can see, no good comes from this kind of attack. Most people simply do not improve when they are repeatedly told they are worthless. No matter what the issue might be, separate the behavior of the person from the person himself.

You might now ask, How is it possible to separate a person's fresh talk or impolite conduct from the person himself? After all, you will insist that what a person does *is* that person. We insist that this is not so. Your behavior is *not* you. Your mate's behavior is not your mate. They are two distinctly separate entities.

Examine for a moment whether or not it is impossible to dislike something about you without also disliking yourself as a person. Can you, for example, dislike your shoes without hating yourself? And if that is possible, it is just as easy to dislike the shape of your ear without damning yourself as a human being. If these two acts are possible, then why can't we also include our behavior? In other words, if you do not like the way you dance, can't you disapprove of your dancing without hating yourself as a human being? The answer is, Of course you can! If you can do this for yourself, can't you also do this for others? In fact, we do this frequently where children or handicapped persons are concerned. Children frequently behave badly, making messes, breaking things, embarrassing us, and we all feel quite irritated at what they do. However, that hardly means that they are worthless or bad. If you do not accept this view, you will wind up being uncontrollably angry with your children and perhaps even beating them. Most beatings are done out of resentment and bitterness in an attempt to get a supposedly bad child to behave well. But the child is not bad, his actions are bad. Why must he and his actions be the same?

There are excellent reasons why we can be most forgiving even though we do not like what happened. Three basic reasons for behavior that we usually regard as bad are: (1) lack of ability to do what is expected, (2) lack of skill and training, (3) emotional disturbance.

1. Let us take as an example a woman who is married to a businessman who is slowly but surely getting up in the world. She comes from a humble, rural background and has never been fully introduced to the sort of life their more affluent friends have adopted. They all play tennis, and tennis, in particular, is something she cannot master. She is grossly uncoordinated and will probably never be able to improve her game because she is so awkward. She loses games and is sometimes laughed at by their friends, although not nearly as much as her husband imagines. He blames her for this deficiency, when in reality there is nothing she can do about it.

In counseling, this woman was told not to allow his accusations to bother her. He was entirely wrong to insist that she was a bad person simply because she was not able to improve her game in order to please him. By the same logic her husband, who is very poor at languages, would have to conclude that he is a worthless person simply because he cannot learn a foreign tongue. This is something that *he* is innately incapable of grasping. No amount of schooling is going to make him a good linguist. Once the woman saw the absurdity of such a position she was better able to accept herself as a decent person even though she remained a poor tennis player. Most of all, she was able to reject her husband's judgment of her even though he still held to it quite firmly. She recognized that this was his problem, not hers.

2. Let us now consider a woman who appears to have good physical coordination but who has never been exposed to intensive tennis and therefore plays badly. What she obviously needs is more practice, many more lessons. In this way she will be able in time to improve her game. Her impatient husband, however, may scold her and blame her for being a poor tennis player. He fails to realize that she has never had the opportunity to practice tennis and therefore has not mastered the game. Again it could be pointed out to the husband that he too is a failure because he does not know how to speak Russian. Yet he obviously cannot be blamed for not speaking Russian if he was never taught the language nor had the opportunity to practice it.

3. Emotional disturbance is the third reason why people will frequently behave badly and for which they should not be blamed. In this case, a woman might have great tennis skills. She has taken lessons for years and has achieved a high degree of perfection in the game. But she sometimes plays badly because she is so intent upon winning that she makes herself nervous. She is not a bad person because she makes herself nervous, she is simply neurotic. Isn't that also an excellent reason to play tennis poorly? How can she possibly play well when she is a bundle of nerves? If she could get hold of herself and learn how to control her anxiety, she would

calm down, use her fine experience and training, and play a decent game of tennis. Until she knows how to get hold of herself, she is bound to play badly simply because she is a disturbed human being, not an evil human being. Therefore, if her husband condemns her *and* her playing, he is nothing less than a fool. It would be no different if the husband were to forget his speech before a business group because of nervousness. He would not be a bad person because he forgot what he wanted to say. He would simply be a disturbed person —that and nothing more. To hate someone for being disturbed is positively absurd and makes no sense whatsoever.

For these reasons blame is never rational. Persons will behave badly some of the time during their lives. We do this simply because we are either unskilled, uneducated, or disturbed. Next time your mate frustrates you in some way that you feel deserves blame, we suggest that you immediately ask yourself why your spouse did this unreasonable thing. He or she must have been incapable, ignorant, or disturbed. These are the reasons why this act was committed, not because your mate is bad. Therefore he or she does not deserve to be hounded, put down, punished, or screamed at. The behavior is *not* the person, and therefore we do not need to damn the entire human being for a few flaws.

"ACCENTUATE THE POSITIVE, ELIMINATE THE NEGATIVE"

If we are literally not to blame those around us whose behavior frustrates us, how do we encourage them to behave in ways that are more acceptable? Are there

methods available that work better than screaming and
badgering? Fortunately there are. Earlier, we sug-
gested that action speaks louder than words. Instead of
a yelling match with your mate over some irritation,
why not simply do something about it? If your wife is
meeting you downtown for dinner and she is late, go
ahead and order without her. That's action, not talk. If
your husband will not pick up his clothes and put them
in the clothes hamper, do not wash them. Don't talk
about it, simply let him run out of clean clothes until he
realizes that no one in the house is going to clean his
clothes until he handles his end of the responsibility.

There is another technique that can perform wonders if you have the patience for it. That technique
comes to us from the learning theory of B. F. Skinner,
the noted Harvard psychologist. He pointed out that
people, animals, earthworms, or whatever, will tend to
repeat behavior if that behavior is rewarded or reinforced. If behavior is not reinforced, it tends to die out.
His theory of shaping human behavior boils down essentially to that simple principle.

Therefore, when you deal with your spouse it is important that you recognize, praise, and reward in some
way all that is good in that person's behavior while at
the same time you *ignore* all that is bad. Sometimes
ignoring the bad behavior while waiting for it to die out
may take too long. Or the irritating behavior may be so
offensive that more immediate steps for dealing with it
are called for. In that case we would suggest that you act
as described above. However, even when you do act,
address your action to the behavior and not to the person. For example, the man who goes ahead and orders
his own dinner because his wife is late can still greet her
with a smile, tell her how good she looks, and assure her

that he would not mind having an extra cup of coffee while she orders her meal. He need say nothing at all about the fact that she is late. In this way he both uses the psychological principle of acting rather than talking and accentuates the positive and eliminates the negative.

To change behavior most efficiently, whether it is in animals, children, or adults, it is important to perform both acts, not just one. In other words, praise your spouse for whatever you find praiseworthy, *and* at the same time do not find fault or be critical. Simply *ignore objectionable* behavior, but *emphasize positive* behavior. Behavior that is not rewarded will truly die out even though it was quite strong at one time. If you have not complimented your wife on her cooking lately, you had better do so now or her zeal for cooking may deteriorate. If you have not complimented your husband on his efforts to provide a good living for the family, for being a diligent worker who faithfully goes to work even when he is not feeling up to it, you had better do so now. If he never gets compliments, he may cease to do so.

Think how lovely it would be if you were treated in this manner. How could you possibly not want to do well for the persons who are continually saying complimentary things to you? Most normal people will respond in kind to the treatment they receive. If they do not, then you can still be considerate and polite to them while making sure that they are not stepping on you or abusing you in some way. This can easily be avoided if you simply do not criticize them but use action instead of talk to show them what you will tolerate and what you won't.

What will happen if you accentuate the positive and

also accentuate the negative? You then strengthen the positive behavior, but you also strengthen some of the negative behavior. The person you are dealing with would then get better in some ways and worse in others. You do not want to accentuate both. Accentuate only the positive and completely ignore the negative if at all possible.

Constant faultfinding, even though it is well intentioned, is one of the most serious detriments to a happy marriage. Where faultfinding persists, there is really no equality in the marriage relationship. One party is constantly seeking domination over the other, or demanding that the mate measure up to the other's expectation.

3

WHAT
IS LOVE?

Undoubtedly love is a term with many meanings, and no simple satisfactory definition has been found. It is thought by some persons to be "something" that mysteriously happens defying rhyme or reason. Others hold the theory of biochemical reaction which suddenly develops a great emotional sensation. Those who believe in this theory feel that it explains the suddenness of falling in love. It is comparable to the chemical reaction of blue mercury solution promptly turning yellow when heated. But the proponents of the theory fail to name the catalyst for the reaction, and we know little more about love than before.

Another viewpoint on how love develops is that it is solely a sexual attraction. No doubt love always starts with such an attraction or slowly develops one. But to reduce love to the level of gratification of a purely physiological urge is to rob it of any spiritual meaning.

What, then, is love and how does it start?

One of the reasons some marriages have difficulties is that people don't know what love is all about. They confuse love with all kinds of romantic ideas. They don't appreciate the fact that love is a logical and businesslike arrangement which happens to be so important that one can get awfully emotional over it. But this does not detract from the fact that love in its final analysis is still very much a mutual affair in which two persons get together and trade favors. It is only when you can see love in this way that you will not feel guilty about standing up for yourself and asking that certain things in your marriage be changed when the need for change arises.

Let's be more precise. Love is that feeling you have for that particular person who can satisfy some of your most important desires. The person you love generally has to satisfy a number of desires, not just one. This is why we do not love all beautiful people. Some of them are not very intelligent and we may also want intelligence in our mates. If we want security, we usually want some other qualities also. That is precisely why a woman who wants security cannot fall in love with just any rich man. When we discover that combination of traits which another person has which pleases us best we tend to fall in love with that person. In other words, we love others because they are who they are, because they can do certain things for us, because *they gratify our desires.* They have the ability to satisfy our deepest and most personal wishes and that is exactly what makes them so attractive to us. It is also what makes so many others in the world neutral to us. Technically, if everyone could satisfy our most basic desires, we would literally fall in love with everyone.

When you say that your love is unselfish and that you would expect nothing from your mate but to be loved in return, you are not speaking very plainly. What you are really saying is that as long as your mate behaves toward you in the very important way that you want to be treated, you will sacrifice and put up with all manner of frustrations from that person because he or she is still satisfying you more than frustrating you. This is why one person can love another even while being mistreated for months or years on end. Apparently the hope that the mate will change is the force that keeps the love alive.

However, when a person becomes convinced that the mate will not reciprocate and the marriage does not satisfy one's deepest expectations, then the marriage is dead. It is no different in business. If you owned a store and hired a clerk who did a good job, you would find her valuable, give her raises, and be warm toward her simply because she is doing what you want her to do. She is making money for you, and she is a decent, pleasant person in the process. However, if your employee began to come to work late, her sales began to drop off, and she was rude to you, you would take steps to change the situation. If this failed, you would simply fire her and be glad to be rid of her. A divorce is no different. It is always an instance where one party says to the other: "You are no longer satisfying my desires, so I am going to be rid of you. You have done a bad job and I want nothing to do with you any longer. Take severance pay and go."

A love relationship and a business relationship are profoundly similar, but there is one difference. In a love relationship we expect to live with this person all of our life. We want to raise children, share our fortunes, have sexual relations, and take vacations together. We usually do not expect this with our business associates. It is only the depths of the relationships, however, not the *nature* of the relationship, which is different. It is perfectly correct to say, when you are in love and plan to marry, that you are going into business with your mate. And as long as each fulfills his or her end of the responsibilities, the business prospers. When the mate does not fulfill the expected role, the business fails.

What each person wants out of a marriage is different, and one person's wants are not more noble than another's. Women generally want affection and security, while men may more frequently seek a family and the conveniences of a regular and safe sex life. For whatever reasons you chose your mate, recognize them for what they are. For example, if you as a woman find yourself strongly attracted to an eligible bachelor who happens to be rolling in money and his wealth has a very definite appeal to you, don't feel guilty about this. Recognize that money is important to you in a marriage. To deny this, if it is true, is simply to blind yourself to an important aspect of your character. You like material things, enjoy travel, desire new clothes, and so on. If that is part of your makeup, there is no reason why you should pretend that it is not so. It is also important then to realize that if you love a man because he has money, you might not love him if he didn't have money. We're not suggesting that you love him *only* because of his money, since we would presume that you also enjoy other things about him, such as his looks, his ability to dance, his tenderness, his ease in social groups. However, if money is one of those important ingredients to you, admit it.

Conflicts in marriage come about precisely because one person has not satisfied the expectations of the other. Communication in the marriage tries to enable both partners to understand what these frustrations are and what can be done to prevent them. Complaints are often expressed in vague and imprecise ways. Persons do not want to appear ill-bred or coarse in insinuating that they are uneasy because they don't have enough money, or are not getting enough sex or attention. The point, however, is that a happy marriage cannot exist unless we face up to the truth of what we want out of a relationship and do not feel guilty about saying so. If we are not inhibited by guilt, we will have little trouble in communicating what it is we want from the other person.

Whenever you do not get what you want from your partner, a little bit of your love dies. When this goes on day after day for months or years, more of your love dies. Eventually the relationship gets to the point where so much of the feeling for the other person has died that no recovery is possible. When your spouse says, "I no longer love you," he or she means, "You have not given me the attention I wanted from you, the tenderness I expected, the financial security I need, or the children I wanted to have." In short, "My personal desires have not been fulfilled and I don't love you because you are not good for me."

That's a coldhearted, businesslike statement, but as we see it, that's essentially the basis of all love relationships. When you are not fulfilling to the other person and he or she is not fulfilling to you (meaning that the two of you won't satisfy each other's desires), you might as well separate.

What we have been referring to above are fairly healthy desires that keep marriages going. However, all of us have been acquainted with marriages that were quite disturbed but the partners still managed to live with each other for years. You may ask, "How is it possible that these people would continue to love each other under such circumstances?"

Let's assume that you see a couple fighting all the time and not separating when it would seem to be the reasonable thing for them to do. You can assume that despite the screaming and bickering they are both satisfying some basic value of each other. For example, suppose a wife thinks very badly of herself. She is convinced she is not as good as other people. She may in fact feel guilty over some past behavior and unconsciously wants punishment in order to repent for her misdeeds. What kind of husband would she choose out of the many men that she might meet? Obviously someone who is going to abuse her and possibly beat her. Therefore, she finds him valuable only as long as he is mean, because she *wants* him to be that way. The marriage is serving a vital purpose to her because it makes her life a living hell. That's what she thought she deserved and that's what she made sure she'd get. To help that marriage it would be wrong simply to stop the husband from abusing her. If this occurred, we might find her getting more disturbed because there would be nobody around to punish her. Instead, we would first try to get her to stop thinking she needs punishment, and then help the husband to modify his behavior. Only when both of those targets were aimed at could there be some hope of lasting peace between them.

The point of this discussion is that these persons can "love each other," according to our definition, even though they are continually embattled. Fundamentally they are still valuable to each other and performing a service, which in this case both of them seem to need.

The same might be said of some wives of alcoholics. Many of these women have a strong mothering complex. Some may even feel neurotically proud of all the suffering they have to put up with. When they look around for husbands, they may select men who are weak and want to be mothered. Therefore, when the man starts to drink and acts like a child, the wife immediately comes to his side and treats him like a misbehaving little boy. He gets scolded and put to bed, but the whole business is essentially tolerated because they both like it. He is supplying her with an important quality she wants: the feeling of being needed. As long as he is a weak, sick human being she feels very important. That's precisely what she is getting out of the relationship. This, of course, is a neurotic value, but all of us who are married have selected our mates for both healthy and unhealthy reasons. If our healthy reasons outweigh our neurotic ones, the chances of making it are better.

Therefore, when you complain to your husband, "All you want from me is my body," don't say it in anger. You may have hit the nail on the head. But what's so wrong with that? One could turn the tables on you and ask, "Why did you marry your husband?" He might say, "All you wanted from me was to be provided for." Is his desiring your body any less worthy than your wanting room and board? We don't see that one person's wants are any more noble or ignoble than the other's. There are, however, more mature reasons for wanting a person, and the more these come into the picture, the better is the outlook for a lasting marriage.

No marriage is purely altruistic. No one gets into this relationship by solely wanting to do someone a favor. Everyone expects something in return, make no mistake about that. You love a person because you are getting your desires fulfilled or you are expecting them to be fulfilled. When these desires are not being fulfilled, there is little reason for the marriage to continue.

To communicate frankly on matters of this kind is extremely difficult. Again the rather dispassionate nature of the written memo may well be the best method to say what should be said.

4

SEXUALITY
IN MARRIAGE

The italic letters in the title are by design. Premarital
or extramarital sex, by its very intent to remain a temporary association, cannot compare to its lasting status
in marriage. The aura of illegitimacy and the thrill of
frequent clandestine meetings carry the seed of excitement and anticipation and may even enhance sexual
relations. On the other hand, marriage in its prosaic
everyday encounter easily reduces sex to routine.

We recall the case of the young, recently married
woman who, soon after the wedding, complained about
pelvic pain. The most thorough examination revealed
no organic causes. Although she still maintained she
loved her husband, she kept rejecting his ardent approaches because of the "pain." After a lengthy and
open discussion she admitted how much better the
premarital relations were because they were "forbidden." She realized that part of the gratification lay in
the revolt against her very strict family upbringing.

There are many sensational books on the market today that give explicit details for every conceivable approach to increasing the sensuality of the love act. They
wrongly encourage the public to believe that the height
of physical love can be obtained by purely technical

accomplishments of the partners. This practice totally overlooks the mystique of physical love, reducing it to a mere mechanical activity. No wonder that followers of this practice often fail.

Between two persons in love a spiritual bond has to be woven with words of tenderness which know neither restraint nor shame. It is impressive how much sensual readiness can be reached by intimate talk, preparatory to the actual love act. The effect on sensuality of fragrances, enticing clothes, subdued lights and romantic music is too well known to elaborate upon.

Husband and wife, in order to overcome staleness of routine in sex, have to be constantly pursuing new ways of physically and mentally expressing their love. Marriage is doomed when one partner, in search of further pleasures, hits a stone wall of false restraint and resistance in the other. There is no such thing as perversion between lovers. Whatever is mutually satisfying, especially if fueled constantly by love, is important for the success of sensual gratification.

THE TWO ENEMIES OF A GOOD SEX LIFE

The two quickest ways in the world to destroy your sex life are to expect perfection in yourself or your partner and to feel guilty about what you want to do sexually.

1. Fear of Failure

If you want to be a good sex partner, then be a relaxed one. Don't try too hard. Don't care too much about how you are doing. Don't insist on being the perfect sexual athlete who makes every occasion an unbelievable experience. If you put these kinds of demands upon yourself, you are going to get nervous about how well you will do and that nervousness may well destroy your effectiveness as a lover. Those who do what comes naturally do a great deal better than those who are striving all the time to be better.

In the actual physical act of making love, this kind of anxiety often causes the man to lose his erection or the woman to become frigid. Because he has had too much to drink, or is too tired, or is bothered by other problems, a man often does not finish the sex act or cannot even get it started. He may begin to worry so much about it that the next time he attempts to make love his mind will be on his previous failures rather than on his wife's physical attractiveness. It would then be nearly impossible for him to perform the sex act adequately.

What we have said about the male applies equally to the female. She too may be trying so hard to have an orgasm that her mind is truly not on sex and its stimulating thoughts but on how awful it would be if she did not succeed or how awful it would be if her husband would find out. One cannot think of something awful and of something charmingly sexy at the same time. So make up your mind. If you want a good sex life, think sex.

You might be asking yourself at this point whether there isn't at least something one can do about satisfying one's partner in the event that erection or lubrication fails. Fortunately, the answer is yes. When you find yourself unwilling or unable to perform the penile-vaginal act for whatever reason, do not despair. Don't deny your partner sexual satisfaction simply because you are not in the mood. Intercourse is a specialized form of sexual activity that leads to orgasm. However, there are other forms of sexual activity that lead to orgasm, or if not to orgasm, then at least to a great deal of pleasure. Manual fondling or petting to orgasm is certainly a very simple, safe, and convenient method of giving your partner sexual satisfaction. It may be necessary to remove the inhibitions that society has built up in us against this kind of sex play before it can be enjoyed without guilt. However, there is no conceivable reason why two persons should not masturbate each other if that happens to be the more convenient direction for their sex activity to take that particular occasion.

Mutual petting or solo petting is enormously important as part of a love act. It is a sensible alternative to normal intercourse when fatigue, menstruation, or illness interfere. In the case of the female, it is obviously completely pregnancy proof. It can provide her with endless orgasms, far more than the male is capable of through intercourse. The male's need to resort to a non-penile method to satisfy his partner is mandatory when he does not have the erect penis available. Petting her to orgasm not only satisfies her but also relieves him of pressure to perform when he does not feel up to it. This effectively removes the threat of failing in the sex act and will help prevent a neurotic fear of impotence. Subsequently, since his mind is not on failure, he does not have to worry. As a result, the normal bodily functions take over and he may find himself with a very healthy desire.

Other techniques are described in the many manuals on marriage that are available, some of which are listed at the end of this book. Our concern is that in this most intimate and personal relationship there is honest communication between the partners. Don't hesitate to share your deepest desires, fears, and expectations with your partner.

2. Guilt

Guilt is the second great enemy of a satisfying and healthy sex life. If you really want to enjoy your bedroom, then do what the two of you find enjoyable. Never mind what your parents told you was proper or improper. What is allowed in sex changes like the fashions. At one time it was thought that sex was proper only when it was intended for procreation. No one takes this seriously any longer. Sex is to be enjoyed as one of those few physical activities in which men and women can engage wholeheartedly and intimately. So enjoy it. You will if you remove all your feelings of guilt about what the two of you are doing.

Nothing that you do to each other sexually is wrong as long as you are not inflicting pain on yourself or on your partner needlessly or without consent. These should be the standards by which you judge your sexual behavior. Don't worry about what the neighbors down the street would think about your sexual behavior if they knew about it. That's none of their business, even if they would be horrified by what you do. What is important, however, is what pleases you and your mate.

Shedding your inhibitions and feelings of guilt is easier said than done. Trying not to feel guilty over acts that all your life you have been brainwashed to believe are wrong takes much effort. Certain notions are much more difficult to counteract than others. In our experience we have found two areas of guilt to be most common: *(a)* having sexual thoughts of someone other than your partner at the time you are engaged in intercourse and *(b)* enjoying sex, especially by being daring and different.

The reason some people are bothered by having thoughts of a person other than their partner stems from their beliefs that simply having an idea is equivalent to having committed the act. It is stressed in some quarters that having lustful thoughts of one person while actually engaging in sex with another is not only inappropriate but downright sinful. This really needs to be questioned. To be a well-functioning sexual person, it is imperative that you keep alive all the passionate imagery that you possibly can. This may include imagining your partner's nude body, what is happening to you physically, remembering lovely past sexual experiences. Good sexual functioning derives from having delicious sexual thoughts. Therefore, any thought that can enhance the pleasure and excitement of the moment will only lead to greater sexual fulfillment and therefore greater pleasure between you and your partner. What does it matter if one of those techniques includes thinking about someone else? That hardly constitutes infidelity, since you cannot commit the act while you are still making love to your mate only. Therefore, next time you are engaged in a passionate sexual embrace and the thought of a different person flashes through your mind, do not allow guilt to spoil all you have both worked for. Enjoy that fleeting pleasure, because it is a harmless one and it is actually adding to the delight of the moment.

Being daring and different in sexual practice also brings out guilt in the timid. The use of certain sexual words, different sexual positions, and possibly the daring use of clothing or the lack of it seem to some to be forbidden and wrong and would suggest that such things should produce guilt. Not so! Any act or practice that could heighten interest in otherwise dull sexual affairs is appropriate and useful if it is not harmful. To resort to more daring techniques, a provocative use of clothing, or expressive language is surely not out of place if both partners enjoy it. Most humans are pleased with variety. In our experience only a minority is really content to do the same activity over and over again in the same way. Although some people may eat pancakes and bacon every morning of their lives or go to bed promptly every night at ten thirty, most of us would find this intolerable. Since we would not approve of a boring routine in other aspects of our lives, why should we tolerate it in our sex lives?

The couple that throw aside the antiquated admonitions that sex is dirty, lust for one's partner is evil, and enjoying sex sinful will enjoy their sex life in ways that other people cannot begin to imagine. These are the liberated people. These are the truly sexually healthy. They do not have irrational inhibitions, regulations, and rules. These are people who have one guiding principle to go by and that is that anything they do between them through mutual consent which is not painful to themselves or others is permissible. They will, therefore, eagerly try new positions, express themselves in blatantly sexual language, show themselves nude with pleasure, or provocatively with revealing clothing. These are the elements of variety that can make some sex lives enormously rich and memorable. Candid communication is again the key to effective practice.

TWO IMPORTANT SEXUAL TECHNIQUES

Constant nearness in marriage sometimes blunts the sex drive. To avoid a decrease in sensuality, husband and wife must be mutually interested in rejuvenating their sex relations with new approaches and stimulations. A desired condition to good sexuality in marriage is, of course, love. Without it, sex is demoted to a mere physical release only devoid of significant emotional depth. Once this important condition, love, has been met, other factors play an important role in achieving orgasmic satisfaction: verbal arousal and erogenous zones.

"Sweet nonsense": that is exactly what you whispered and liked to hear during courtship. It is a powerful aphrodisiac and remains one for all times. The trouble is that we forget the power of words to fire up our imaginations. Physicians and psychologists have strongly recommended the use of preparatory erotic language as part of the foreplay to intercourse. Complimentary, amorous talk and sex-oriented conversation have frequently changed the receptiveness of many a reluctant woman or man. An excellent example is offered in the story of Cyrano de Bergerac. His romantic and passionate letters changed a shy maiden's feeling into an intense yearning for the unknown lover. Prolonged and intimate conversation can arouse sensuality as such words release the innermost feelings.

This art, so practiced in courtship, must not be discarded in marriage. On the contrary, more of it is necessary to provoke a sensual response. Talking about sex, reading an erotic book together, or recalling previous ecstatic hours are all apt to rekindle a fading desire. To woo is the name of the game and the more years that have passed since the wedding day, the more that tender words are needed to create a sensual mood.

An overardent husband, still grimy and sweaty from work, can hardly expect an enthusiastic response from his wife when he returns home. The tired husband, deep in thought about a professional problem, will need more than direct sexual opportunity in order to be ready for the overtures of his wife. We remember the story of a housewife whose husband considered it his right to assault her daily after work as soon as he entered the house. In the beginning he had the decency at least to remove his work boots; later, even that was too much of an effort. It is no wonder she hated to see him drive into the driveway. In the end she ran away. He is still wondering why. "I gave her so much love, that ungrateful bitch!" he lamented.

Sensitive marital partners are always aware of each other's mood. Lead up to sex gently. Take time to let emotions arise. You may see your tired husband turn into a wild lover and your bored wife become a passionate mistress.

Much has been said and written about this theme. The range of literature extends from simple facts to the most sophisticated explanations. Some books leave the ludicrous impression that the body is divided into responsive and nonresponsive areas. We are given a map by which we are supposed to be guided to the correct erogenous locations. Such naïveté is shocking. Other books expand the physiological description of the sexual act until it reads like a lesson in anatomy.

Basically, all of the body is sensitive, with some areas

richer in nerve endings than others. This fact per se does not make them more erogenous. For instance, the tips of the fingers are the most sensitive part of the hand, yet they are not receptive to sexual stimulation. Only the mental process associated with what we touch and feel with the fingers creates the condition of sensuality. By using the hand, we transmit pleasure to someone else, particularly if *guided by the partner* to the preferential zones. The natural instinct to want such thrills is only interfered with by false modesty, shame, and embarrassment. One woman, after twenty-five years of marriage, finally admitted having pleasurable sensations when touched at specific spots. By that time many years had been lost and many barriers erected which precluded a satisfactory sexual relation between her husband and herself. There is no doubt that the sexual satisfaction of one partner when expressed in words, movements, or exclamations is a powerful stimulant to the other. The desires of love and sex want to be recognized and rewarded, otherwise they retreat in embarrassed inactivity. Man's virility in particular expects a woman's sighs of satisfaction as proof of his prowess, no doubt a childish remnant of the culture of male dominance. So, women, let yourselves go! Make your husband happy, and free yourself of inhibitions also.

The primary erogenous zones are the clitoris of the female and the glans (the head of the penis) of the male. A secondary area of intense sensitivity is the nipple of a woman's breast. Besides these, any other spot on the skin can arouse a sexual desire depending on the individual's preference. The most important secondary erogenous zone is the lips. That is why kissing is an excellent way to arouse sensual desire. Obviously oral hygiene and dental care have a great influence on the pleasure derived from kissing. Even the best perfume cannot replace a clean and fresh mouth. Many a lover has been turned off by careless hygienic habits. Bad odors can repulse the most ardent advances.

The number of ways in which sexual desires can be stimulated is endless, and some of them are quite unusual. As long as both partners mutually agree and enjoy the variations of lovemaking, there is nothing perverse about them. Probably the most common missing element in marriage is foreplay. During courtship, lovemaking contains the elements of seduction, and ardent effort to woo and win. After the wedding, though, this effort is minimal or missing. Nothing will cool a woman's receptiveness for love more quickly than matter-of-fact sex without precoital tenderness. For most women the foreplay is an integral part of their sexual communication with the partner. Any shortcut will lessen a woman's self-esteem and thus impair her full satisfaction. She feels she has not been loved, but has been used. The "hit and run" type of lover belongs in movies and James Bond thrillers. Frequently a woman's urging to her partner to hurry up is not a sigh of extreme and impatient desire, but the exact opposite—the desire to get it over! The impatient, virile male may be the poorest lover. Let this be a warning to men to remain humble where sex is concerned.

Humanity was made to enjoy sex. When it is not a joy, something is wrong in the relationship. Perhaps acquired inhibitions interfere with natural desire and sexual aggressiveness. Guidelines for erotic behavior, positions, technique, and skills can only be what they claim to be: guidelines. The end result of a pleasurable experience therefore lies with you and how freely and honestly you decide to communicate sexual matters with your mate. If something bothers you and you can't talk about it, try writing a memo.

5

OTHER COMMON AREAS OF CONFLICT

THE REARING OF CHILDREN

"Johnny, I told you not to do that," the irate mother impatiently screamed at her six-year-old son. To emphasize her displeasure, she gave him a resounding smack on the seat. The ensuing crying, which filled the house to the farthest corner, brought Father on the scene. "What's going on here? Can't I work in peace? Why do you always beat the child?"

The stage is set for one of those quarrels based on impatience and a lack of knowledge of the facts. When Dad came home Junior was just perfect. Not only did Junior enjoy having a new face around after a whole day with Mother, but he was smart enough to put his best foot forward. Although Dad was a good deal sterner than Mother when it came to discipline, he saw nothing here that called for stern measures. In the eyes of the father the boy was just a "cute, lively kid," as boys should be. But what Father did not know was that the boy had broken a valuable plate, torn his pants climbing a fence, and dragged dirt from the yard all over the clean carpets. He had been reprimanded by Mother several times. Finally she lost her temper when he added one more trick from his inexhaustible repertoire.

The above case shows how not to handle the rearing of children. The smart youngster learned early how to play one parent against the other. The breach in the common parental front was cleverly used to his advantage. This situation can be avoided when parents discuss beforehand the upbringing of their children. A common goal has to be worked out and practiced by both parents. Children want authority and like to be guided. This does not mean the whip, or an exactly prescribed schedule leaving the child without any possibility of self-expression. Overdisciplined children will revolt, and overprotected ones will become weaklings.

A frequent family dispute concerns a boy's participation in sports. The father wants his boy to get into football and slug it out. The mother tries to prevent her little son from being exposed to injury. This situation shows a total lack of communication between the parents in regard to the aspirations for their children. Quarreling about it in the presence of the child will make a bad situation even worse. For the sake of the children, parents must present a united front. They should resolve their differences in private conversation and spare the child from conflicting standards.

There are two neglected disciplines in the teaching of men and women: marriage and parenthood. Schools offer endless hours in specialized studies. Skills are taught in adult classes from arranging flowers to self-defense. Everything, it seems, can be learned except being husbands and wives, and fathers and mothers. In these two disciplines we stubbornly insist upon learning by experience, by success and failure.

The rearing of children in particular has been badly neglected. Even the worst parents seem surprised when their offspring do not turn out well. "Where did I fail?" the heartbroken parents wail. If they are honest, they have to admit that they took little time for the education of their children. It is generally assumed that being a good father or mother is a God-given faculty and no teaching is necessary. Yet modern society is fraught with obstacles for the adolescent who, more than ever, needs the guiding hand of parents.

A married couple who have differing views on how to bring up their children will constantly pull in opposite directions. The outcome is psychological bedlam for the poor youngster. The misunderstanding between the parents will finally spill over into other spheres of their relationship. From the very beginning the treatment of children should remain uniform, and open rifts among parents must be avoided. Discord over the methods of rearing a child can lead to marked disturbance of harmony in marriages that otherwise were good.

THE FOUR REASONS FOR MISBEHAVIOR

Some of the most heated arguments between married persons occur over the rearing of children. Now that psychology and psychiatry have studied children for years, there are insights and understandings that could be helpful.

We find that children misbehave for one or more of the following four reasons. They want (1) attention, (2) power, (3) revenge, or (4) responsibility.

1. Desire for Attention

When a child disrupts adult conversation, makes noise when company comes, misbehaves the minute a third party enters the room, he is an attention getter. Instead of you and your mate jumping at each other about the child's poor behavior, just assume that one or both of you have given him too much attention and have unwittingly trained him to act like a prima donna. You may have done this by spending a lot of time scolding him when it would have been much wiser simply to *ignore* him. That's the best way to cure an attention getter. If he will not desist, send him to his room and let him remain there until he is satisfied that no one is going to pay attention to him. If it takes several hours, so be it. If he begins to wreck the room, have him go to a room he cannot wreck. Put him in the basement until he calms down. Be united in this. Do not spend much time preaching to the child. Simply avoid him or isolate him, first only a few minutes at a time, but later for much longer if necessary.

2. Desire for Power

When a child is in a power struggle with you he is trying to prove that he is stronger than you are. We are of course not referring to physical strength in this instance but to the power that you have to make him do what he does not want to do.

The wise parent will recognize that the child is correct. It is the child who is more powerful than the parent, because the child is ruthless and rash in the length to which he will go in order to win. It is hoped that a parent will not cut off his nose to spite his face, but a child does this all the time. Because he does so he wields enormous power. For example, if you say to your child that he must do his homework, he can easily prove to you that he is more powerful than you are by daydreaming. You certainly cannot make a child do homework, or make him learn, or make him graduate from school if he does not want to. He has you over the barrel and you are a wise parent if you admit it. These are insights into facts of life which both parents will want to talk over a number of times or express in memos to each other so that they can come to a common understanding.

It is best to avoid a power struggle from the start. If, however, you do find yourself in one, back off and simply say to your child: "I am sorry that I thought I was going to make you do something. I know I can't make you do what you don't want to do. You are more powerful than I am. Therefore, if you want to flunk out of school, flunk. You'll get a poor job for your efforts. If you want to keep your room dirty, I can't stop you. However, you won't be allowed to have guests in your room until it is clean. I cannot stop you from dropping your clothes on the floor. But if you want them washed, you will have to pick them up and put them in the hamper. I cannot make you wash the dishes. However, if you want to eat from dishes in this house, you will have to wash them. The choice is yours."

3. Desire for Revenge

Revenge, the third reason why children misbehave, only results after the child has learned to hate people and wants to hurt them. He usually learns this from his friends, from his experiences in school, and sometimes from his parents or other members of the family. If you want to stop a child from hating other people, you will have to learn how to love him despite his poor behavior.

To do this, you will want to distinguish between the child's behavior and the child himself. Tell him that you frequently do not like his actions, although that has nothing to do with your feelings toward him as a human being. If he can learn to accept himself as he is and never blame himself for whatever he does (even though he must hold himself responsible for what he does), you will find that he will be a much easier person to live with.

A person and that person's behavior are *not* the same. When we blame ourselves or blame others, we are committing an immoral act. We are all just imperfect human beings who are trying to get through life as best we can. Therefore, we can expect to do bad things periodically even though we may try very hard not to. We are not being evil, we are simply being human. This sort of distinction can save us from becoming hateful toward our own child, and he in turn will not seek revenge.

4. Desire for Responsibility

The child who is pleading illness and weakness so that he does not have to grow up must be handled, not with shouting and instruction, but simply with more responsibility. Let him sweat through whatever trial and error he must, and do not give him so much help that he is delivered out of his problem. We learn through frustration and pain. Helping a child to avoid the pain involved in learning hurts him immeasurably in the long run. Therefore, if your boy wants to stay home from school because he has a stomachache, put him to bed. Pull the drapes, deny him the television or the radio, all books and magazines. Tell him very nicely that this is where he will have to stay until he feels better. Do not allow him to have company when the children come home that night, and in all likelihood, if he is a normal child who does not have a neurotic fear of school, he will no doubt get better very quickly. Whenever you are too helpful, you are not being helpful at all.

You and your mate will have a number of differences in the approach you take to your rearing of children. Rather than argue each difference, put your views down on paper. Think them out carefully so that you can learn about how each of you sees your role as a parent. If communicating with these memos does not do everything you would like it to do, read all the books on the subject you can. If problems persist, by all means get professional help.

RELATIVES

Interfering in-laws, well-meaning friends, and nosy relatives: this is the phalanx that newlyweds often have to break or circumvent. It is a formidable force to face, and only the united front of husband and wife can protect the privacy of marriage.

It is difficult enough for newlyweds to adjust to each other's habits and life-styles without having to carry the albatross of their families around their necks. Ideally husband and wife owe their first loyalty to each other. Yet love and respect for parents, and memories of protected childhood, cannot be put aside easily, nor should they be. Basically there is no competition between those two emotions: love for the mate and love for parents. Still, sometimes a not-so-silent struggle goes on between in-laws and a newly acquired mate. It results in an emotional tug-of-war which, to say the least, can be nerve-racking. Accusations such as, "Your mother keeps interfering" or "Yours is not much better, always insinuating I was not good enough for you," are commonplace. An endless stream of accusations, many of them fabricated in the heat of the argument, obscure the true facts. It is time then to sit down and write the memo.

If, for instance, the problem is that you find yourself always going to your mate's relatives for the holidays or on vacations and you dislike this, then by all means say so. Your partner is not going to know what you really feel unless you talk up about it fairly strongly. You needn't do it in an angry way, but you should do it in no uncertain terms. Do not feel guilty about insisting upon your mate's loyalty. You have a right to expect to be number one and not play second fiddle to parents and relatives.

One major reason why a marriage partner will put the first family before the second is the feeling of guilt and obligation toward parents. That means that he or she feels uneasy for denying them their wishes and putting the mate in first place. Perhaps the mother-in-law cannot fully accept the fact that her son is married and has new obligations. She expects the same devotion from him that he gave her when he was still unmarried. The husband and son who has not broken the tie to his family to a reasonable degree will be very uncomfortable about disappointing his mother. He will try to pacify her—a mistake that is bound to multiply in due course. As we mentioned before, we should not feel responsible for other people's disturbances. It is his mother, in this case, who has the problem. She will have to work on growing up and realizing that her son has another family.

If she indirectly makes him feel sorry for her and guilty for her loneliness, she practices emotional black-mail. When a family controls a member of a marriage it often does so through this means. In effect the family is saying, "You are responsible for our unhappy state of mind."

Here is a wealth of material that a husband and wife could discuss or put down in writing if speaking to each other causes too much of an emotional involvement. If you can bring the right interpretation to light and let the marriage partner see how this situation looks to you, the offending behavior may change. By your calm writ-ten message and simple explanation your mate will gain insight into what is disturbing you.

I recall the case of the very pretty wife who rejected her brother-in-law, making her husband quite angry with this attitude. Later it was established that the brother had attempted to fondle her in a most unbroth-erly fashion. Her desire to avoid an unpleasant situation almost caused a bitter separation between husband and wife. It is not necessary to be approved of by everyone. As long as you are not being hated by someone, you have reason to feel secure. It is time that we realize how much more serious it is to be hated than not to meet approval. This sort of rejection is harmless unless we allow it to affect our egos, but hatred can be quite seri-ous and lead even to bodily injury. Therefore, the diffi-culties you have with the in-laws or the misunderstand-ings with your family that develop after marriage may

well be irritating, but they are not usually vital issues to
your ultimate well-being.

FRIENDS

We do not choose our families. The family provides
the surroundings we are born into and grow up in, and
the characteristics we inherit. It is part of us and we can
never really divorce ourselves from it. Friends, though,
are chosen.

A married couple have two kinds of friends: those
they have in common, and those each has individually.
The first are usually selected by mutual agreement.
They are the ones who suit both parties because of a
common interest, social standing, and other factors.
These friends can be changed easily without it causing
much of an emotional disruption in their everyday
lives. A personal friend, however, comes into marriage
like a dowry and willy-nilly has to be taken in even if not
always acceptable to the mate. Since real friends are
rare, it would be a mistake for a mate to insist that such
personal friends be dropped.

We recall the story of a young woman who had enjoyed lifelong friendship with another girl. In due
course this friend was divorced. From then on she lived
the life of a modern liberated woman. The husband of
the young wife, fearing the bad influence of that friend,
tried in every way possible to break up this friendship.
Though he had no reason whatsoever to suspect any
interference from her in their marital life, he kept harp-
ing on the subject persistently. As a matter of fact, no
attempt was ever made by this woman to persuade the

wife to live as she lived. There was certainly no need for the husband to play the role of guardian of his wife's virtue. She had done well without him in the years before. The friendship between the two women continued and is still going strong. Unfortunately the husband never came to terms with his own personal hang-up about this friendship.

Since this was an emotionally loaded subject, an exchange in writing, as suggested by the Memo Method, could have revealed the in-depth reasonings of both partners and saved a lot of unnecessary quarreling and bickering.

RELIGION, POLITICS,
AND PHILOSOPHY OF LIFE

One of the most disruptive forces in the world is prejudice, and a frequent form of prejudice involves religion. This fact can become especially damaging in marriages with mixed religious background.

Differences in religious beliefs may not seem relevant to newlyweds who are still unconcerned about the future. The situation changes later. As time goes by, initial tolerance tends to decrease and, unless carefully watched, religion can become a seriously disruptive force. Frequently parents try to influence the couple to accept the tradition to which they are loyal, and at least to promise to raise the children in that tradition. Yet, even without such interference the choice of which religion to adopt must come up once children are born. In which faith shall the children be raised? Which holidays will be observed? The ultimate decision must be made after thorough discussion between husband and wife, since it will affect the future life of the family. Once their minds are made up, there should be no room for wavering or belated reservations.

Here is an example of religious difficulties that arose as early as the courting stage. Two young people fell in love. He was Jewish and she came from a devout Catholic home. Love temporarily had wiped out all prejudices and they looked forward to a happy marriage. The parents though did not agree that easily with the choice. The Catholic parents did not want their daughter to marry the Jewish boy, and the mother of the boy could not accept the Gentile girl. Reared in such surroundings and nourished since early childhood with such attitudes, the children can hardly be expected to remain unaffected by this education. Though the youth of today grow up thinking for themselves, they cannot free themselves totally from the preconceived ideas that prevail in the parental home. The two young people mentioned thought that love would conquer all obstacles and decided to go ahead and marry nevertheless.

As a compromise they became Unitarians, though neither of them understood or knew anything about this denomination. Not having the courage to face parental objections, they opted for a religious background unknown to either of them, leaving it to their children one day to make their own choices. The end result was a lukewarm religious affiliation, with both mates unhappy about it but not daring to say so. In the long run the stronger partner determined the religious life to be practiced in the home and by which the children would be raised, against the slow-burning resentment of the mate. The future of this couple's marriage is uncertain. One day, when other reasons for misunderstandings will arise, the religious question may become explosive.

Another typical example of a religious conflict is the clash over family planning. A young man wanted a vasectomy because he was not earning the kind of money he thought was needed to raise more than three children. He was in his early thirties and already felt fairly inadequate. He did not want to have more responsibilities placed on top of what he already had. His wife was very much against it because of her religious convictions. She threatened divorce if he went ahead with this move. Although at first the idea of the operation went against his religious and moral principles too, he rethought the issue and satisfied himself that it would be wrong to bring any more children into the world. If his wife seriously disapproved of his action, he simply would have to leave her, because this was one of those issues on which he was not ready to compromise, no matter what.

There was considerable arguing between them on this matter, but one day the husband put his words down on paper and spelled out exactly how he felt about the whole issue. He let his wife know his fears of taking on more responsibility. He made it clear that he was determined to leave her if she objected to the operation. For the first time she clearly saw where he stood and what motivated him. It was up to her either to accept her husband's vasectomy and compromise her own religious principles or to remain firm and separate from him. In this instance she gave in, allowed him to have the vasectomy, and things worked out quite well.

You will occasionally face issues on which you cannot or will not compromise. It is extremely important then to stand pat. If you give in time after time, you may find yourself unhappy with the compromise you have made.

You will hold your mate responsible for the misery it caused you. This is the way married couples build up grudges. They do favors for their mates by not protesting too much at the time a decision was made. Charitably they give in and sacrifice their own principles for the sake of marital harmony. However, when this goes on time after time and year after year the person who has given in builds up resentment. There will come a time when silence is no longer golden, and bitter complaints about all the sacrifices that had to be made will be made. This is a regrettable waste of energy. Five years later, five days later, or even five minutes later is too late to complain about something that you have allowed previously. It is much better to take a firm stand that supports your life's philosophy even if, for the moment, it may cause tension.

Have your differences out and have them out immediately. Do not give in out of a sense of love and then blame the other person for what you have already allowed to happen. This is monstrously unfair and produces nothing but increased hostility in the long run. It makes you indirectly angry because you allowed yourself to be manipulated, while this change of relationship indirectly makes your mate hostile because he or she feels betrayed.

Get your pencil out when you feel objections coming on. Express them as honestly and as politely as you can. Do not wait!

ECONOMICS AND FINANCES

Early in life we are taught mathematics in order to cope with certain problems. We use figures to tell time, to balance books, to plan activities and travel, and for hundreds of other things. Indeed, figures have become so important that without them life would be chaotic.

Once we are married, the life needs of another person enter into the calculations. And more than this; because the two are married, joint needs emerge and the independence of each is to some degree necessarily restricted. All of a sudden we are faced with the fact that we must account to another person for what we do and particularly how we spend our money. This restriction, though voluntary, is bound to create tension and misunderstanding. This is particularly so when communication is not good and common problems are not mutually discussed.

Economics and financial affairs often create stumbling blocks in the otherwise smooth-running life of a married couple. More than in any other sphere, tact and understanding are required for working out these problems to the satisfaction of both partners. Thrift by one partner may badly rub against the urge to spend of the other. Since there is never enough money, friction easily develops. The way a person handles money is largely influenced by family background, past economic experience, and personal attitude toward security and pleasure.

The difference will increase or abate the longer the marriage lasts. Budgeting for items such as clothing, vacations, or the acquiring of property fares better when mutually agreed upon. With the liberation of women, the wife more than ever has become a partner in vital decisions which years ago were the sole domain of men. Even a tight budget should permit an occasional splurge, a surprise gift, or a luxurious vacation. Without these rare excursions into the world of "dreams come true" life would be boring and monotonous. The clever couple will economize for these rare expenses. The memory of a common pleasurable experience will more than compensate for the extra cost it entails.

The use of possessive pronouns in marriage is often significant. "This is mine" and "That is yours" sometimes creates the notion that two separate units exist rather than one. We hold that each partner shall be responsible for common needs, yet have a certain amount of money for personal use without having to account for how it is spent. There is something radically wrong if one partner cannot trust the other.

When it comes to investments, they should be discussed by both mates. In spite of all precautions, mistaken judgment and subsequent loss in investments are bound to occur. To harp on the loss and put the blame on the other marriage partner will undoubtedly lead to ugly quarrels. Therefore, do not scold when the stocks do badly. Do not blame the one who does the shopping for extravagance if you have not been in a supermarket lately.

A good example of how a quarrel over financial affairs can disturb an otherwise contented marriage is seen in the story of the store owner who kept buying stocks on tips. Whenever he succeeded, his wife demeaned the successful transaction with remarks such as, "Anybody who reads *The Wall Street Journal* could do it." This belittling did not sit well with the husband. The acrimony got even worse when the tips did not work out and he lost on the stock market. Then the blame was always put squarely at his door—it was his carelessness, his inability to read company reports, his rash judgment that caused the loss.

After many harangues the husband simply shut up like a clam and never again mentioned any stock deals he had made. Of course the wife would not believe that he had stopped investing. She accused him of lying to her. The harassment carried over to other areas in their lives. What started as a harmless disagreement on economic matters deteriorated into a miserable marital state. At the time of this writing they are still at it!

VACATIONS, ENTERTAINMENT, SPORTS, HOBBIES

"The family that plays together stays together" is a cliché that carries a great truth. Common activities create a strong bond between partners. Common interests, though not the cement of a lasting relationship, can be the spice that flavors it. The thrill of a joint experience, the excitement of a sporting event, or just the togetherness of watching a beautiful sunset can create a special warmth between husband and wife. The emphasis is on "joint experience" and "voluntary" participation. Nothing could be worse than to drag a reluctant partner along who would rather be doing something else. The easy give-and-take of the early days in marriage can be replaced by a rigid attitude of a mate who is not ready to make any sacrifice of personal comfort or preferences toward the pleasure of the other.

On the other hand, why should two individuals reared in different backgrounds have the same tastes and aspirations? Obviously, they do not. The trick is not to find the partner with the exact same outlook on vacations or hobbies and sports, but to meet the one who is willing to attempt to share at least some common interests. By exploring the differences, a husband and wife are bound to develop some common likings they were not aware of having had before.

We recall the couple whose yearly vacation was a painful experience as long as it was planned according to the husband's wishes. Finally he realized that a grumpy, unhappy wife was no asset to a good time. From then on they mapped their vacations together to please them both. Writing down their wishes and objections greatly helped.

Entertainment is another sore point in many marriages. "I would not be caught dead listening to an opera," the husband exclaims, as he tears up the ticket his wife bought. Giving him tit for tat, the wife proceeds to put a match to the admission ticket for the football game. Can you imagine the ensuing quarrel? Still, that's what happens with variations in many marriages.

It makes no difference really whether the preferred form of pleasure is sophisticated music or a boisterous party in a smoke-filled tavern. When enjoyed together, each happening becomes something to talk about and relive in the future. This does not mean that one partner has to renounce a favorite pastime in favor of the other's. The well-adjusted couple will not mind being separated while each follows preferred hobbies and sports. But nothing more unites two people in love than to explore together. It reminds us of the couple who had successfully completed an art course in painting. Originally it was the husband who had dabbled in oil for years and was "the expert." It took quite a lot of talking to convince the wife to join the same course. In the end it turned out that she was the more talented artist. Needless to say, they went to many more classes, exhibits, and museums afterward. What started as a compromise ended in a mutually happy experience that drew the couple still closer together.

To cut short any verbal objections from your mate to your proposal for a different approach to vacation or fun, write it down. The memo will give your mate ample time to think about it and to respond thoughtfully. Compromise is not weakness but a sign of respect for the other mate, an important ingredient for a successful marriage.

6

EXAMPLES
OF THE MEMO METHOD

The following is an example of the Memo Method at
work. Read the wife's communiqué as though it were
handed to you by your mate. Then put the book down
for a moment and ask yourself whether you fully understand what is being said and how the communication
itself could be immensely improved. You will find our
observations of the problem under "Discussion and
Analysis" and the way we handled it. It is our hope that
this method, which, we are convinced, is a superior way
to communicate, will be helpful to you in dealing with
problems in your marriage.

THE MEMO METHOD AT WORK

This woman felt desperate about her husband's domi-
neering ways, because she was raised by a mother and
father who were also dictatorial. Although she was passive in her marriage for the first seven years, she finally
got to the point where she could not tolerate this any
longer. She began to rebel. She has told her husband a
great many times the sort of things that she has written
about here. He still came on strong, trying to run her

life particularly when he felt she was being unwise. His motives were loving in nature, but the moment he took on a fatherly attitude and tried to control her in what he regarded as foolish behavior, she saw red. She transferred emotional responses from her father and mother onto her husband and the marriage suffered for days on end. The two of them came for marital counseling, and as an exercise in getting each one to understand the gist of the frustration of the other, they were asked to write down their thoughts in a communiqué, as espoused in this book. So strong is the habit of pouring forth ideas as they come into one's head that the wife completely forgot to put down the problem, the cause, and the proposed solution. Instead we have the following:

"I love you, but I need to be my own person. I don't need criticism. For example, the night you said that sexual relations were so very important to me when I wasn't living at home, this hurt me for one very important reason. My mother continually called me a two-bit whore and she continually told me how worthless I was. After I married you, you continually held this over my head. I don't need any more of this kind of treatment. I am a good, intelligent, and caring person. And no matter what decisions I have made I am still me. I deserve respect. I've worked for it and I have tried to give it to others. I gave more to you than any one and I will not allow myself to be put down again. I don't know why you have to put me down like you did that Saturday night. You expect me to leave you alone, trust you, and help you. Well, I need just as much consideration. I have a lot of hurt to overcome and a lot of life to live. I realize you do too. But I heard over and over again, 'Help me, help me,' from you and what did I get? Did you ever think that if I had gotten what I needed and if I had felt wanted and loved that none of this would ever have happened?

"People have been willing to use me. You used me. Well, I will be used no longer. I want our relationship to work. I will work very hard on it but not just on your terms. I do love you and I want it to work out."

Discussion and Analysis

This statement says a number of things rather eloquently. We get the feeling that this girl has been put upon by her husband because she has allowed him to dominate her as she was dominated by her parents. However, why could this simply not have been said straightforwardly in one or two sentences such as the following:

PROBLEM: You have dominated me all our married life, just like I allowed my father and mother to dominate me.

Here is the problem in a nutshell. We do not have to sift through a page and a half of writing to find out what it is that truly irks her. All we need to do is look under the heading PROBLEM, and we immediately know where we stand.

Her note gives us no clear indication of why her husband continually pushes her around. We know this happens, that she dislikes it a great deal, but not why it happens. This is exactly why a section on CAUSE is so valuable. Had she taken time to analyze this question she might have given her husband some valuable information. For example, she might have indicated something like this as the cause:

"You like to push me around because it makes you feel big."

"You might do this because you have a problem with your father and mother and have adopted some of their pushy tactics."

"You think you have to have everything you want, and, like a child, get angry when you are frustrated."

"You may foolishly think that I enjoy being dominated because I am a woman and that you are being good to me because I want a big, strong he-man."

Whatever the reason, this was not explored in her communication to him at all. She simply states that she resents being treated badly and that she is a good person who does not deserve it. That is about all. Her message, in fact, becomes a vehicle for her to ventilate a great deal of feeling, which, in and of itself, is not bad, but it is not particularly informative.

She offered no reasons for the causes of this problem and she also offered no solutions. All she did was to tell him that his behavior had to stop, but she gave him no indication as to *how* it might stop. She did not recommend any books for him to read, did not suggest that they take a vacation together, that he leave her alone whenever she gets mad, and so on. This means that her communication was a vehicle for expressing her feelings but was not a vehicle for solving her problems. Even if the husband wanted to help his wife, he would be hard put to do so since he does not know what is causing the problem and what he ought to do to stop it. If he is to follow his wife's advice, he will simply have to develop a lot of willpower, grit his teeth, fly by the seat of his pants, and do something without understanding why he ought to do it or what alternatives he might have to simply desisting a form of behavior which she finds intolerable.

Perhaps this case demonstrates the necessity for being rather logical and careful in thinking your problems through. Do not use your marriage memo as a way of telling someone off. Use it as a way of cementing a relationship. Letting your feelings flow is perfectly fine in its proper place. However, when one tries to be constructive, that is no time to be neurotically emotional and bitter. What this person has done is to put in writing the same sort of things that she has been saying to her husband all along. To a degree this may be healthy, but it is not the stuff out of which good communication comes. Otherwise they would not be having these problems, since she has told him these things time and time again. A good marriage memo does more than tell the other partner of one's feelings. It states the nature and the origin of the problems and offers possible solutions.

In the pages that follow, you will see numerous examples of the Memo Method. Some are samples from our practice, and we have been given permission to use them. Others are paraphrases of conversations we have had with our clients.

THE MEMO METHOD APPLIED
TO PROBLEMS OF LOVE

PLAINTIFF: The Wife Who Needed More Conversation

PROBLEM: I had a bad day at work and waited to be cheered up by you. But you started talking about your troubles and never bothered to listen to me.

Cause 1: You make such a big thing out of your problems that you honestly believe after a while that no one has difficulties but you.

> SOLUTION 1: Why not try challenging your habit of making mountains out of molehills all the time? We've been over and over this before and you still aren't learning that most of the things you get excited about never seem to happen. By seriously questioning your whole assumption that the world is going to come to an end, you might calm down enough to be able to get off your problems for a while and listen to someone else's.

Cause 2: I suspect that you feel you must be the center of attention because you are an only child and always had all the attention you wanted.

> SOLUTION 2: I am afraid I am going to have to be more aggressive and break into your conversations at times and simply force you to hear what I have to say. It isn't your fault that you were trained to be the star attraction, and I don't want to blame you for this problem. However, I want some attention paid to my problems at times. If you can't see it, then I really must be more forceful when bringing it to your attention.

REPLY

DEFENDANT: The Husband

> PROBLEM: You continually refuse to realize that I am tired of listening to people all day long. When I get home I shut you out in the same way I shut out everyone else.

Cause 1: I think you still have an immature streak in you which makes you think you have to have your way and that whatever I do is done to affront you personally.

SOLUTION 1: Give me half an hour to unwind when I get home. Don't tell me about any problems or troubles until after dinner. I'd rather hear pleasantries first.

SOLUTION 2: Prepare yourself for my silence when I come home. Remind yourself of this quirk of mine *before* I get home and you'll not be annoyed anymore.

SOLUTION 3: Read a book on how to control your anger, or get counseling for that purpose.

Discussion and Analysis

Being listened to is an enormously rewarding experience, and when one person in marriage is neglected in this respect, the whole marriage suffers. The wife is correct in bringing this neglect to the attention of her husband, and we can see that the husband has communicated some important information to her from which she can profit. She does not have to take his behavior personally, she learns, because he must do a great deal of listening on his job and is counting upon her to let him unwind when he gets home.

He has avoided some of the issues that she has raised, thereby indicating to her that he does not agree with them. Should she care to pursue them further, then let her discuss them through another memo or simply work it out in a discussion over a cup of coffee as they compare notes.

It should be appreciated that some of these remarks, if they had been made verbally, could have set off a flurry of protests. Having them in writing, however, gives the reader the opportunity to think over at leisure what point is being made, and whether or not it is a valid one. Then, when the couple get together to discuss the issues, they will have settled down and will be ready to deal with them in an unemotional way.

PLAINTIFF: The Wife Who Felt Rejected

PROBLEM: Before it used to be, "I love you," a dozen times a day. You have not said it once for the last month.

Cause 1: Have you fallen out of love with me and can't say, "I love you," anymore?

SOLUTION 1: If I have disillusioned you, there must be a reason. And if you tell me about it, I will try to better myself. Have I failed sexually, or do I not live up to your expectations as a companion? Teach me, but don't reject me or pout. I am a good pupil if given a chance.

Cause 2: Is there something about me that angers you? Have I changed? If so, I am not aware of it and talking to me would clear up the misunderstanding.

SOLUTION 2: We are not children anymore and should be able to take criticism. It's true I was preoc-cupied lately with the arrangements for the club anniversary and did not pamper you as before. This must not be a reason for you to become cold. I shall gladly tell you all about my activities and I want you to participate. Would that change your attitude?

Cause 3: I imagine that after being married awhile the bloom is gone. What upsets me is the sudden change that has come over you. Is there another woman?

SOLUTION 3: I imagine marriage shows off the bad side of mates and sometimes love becomes old hat. I suspect you of having another woman, but shall not try to follow you or snoop. That's beyond my dignity. I can take the truth even if that is what caused the sudden freeze. True, I love you, but love is a two-way street. Remember!

REPLY

PROBLEM: You trust words more than deeds. I've done nothing to give you cause to think I'm rejecting you, yet you always want to hear me say, "I love you."

Cause: In your family talk was cheap. I think they fooled each other with sweet words most of the time but went ahead being unfair to one another in deeds.

SOLUTION: Don't put so much stock in my verbal reassurances. Of course I love you and I want to express that in words at times. But if I don't say it as often as you like, then it's you who have become touchy. Furthermore, my behavior gives you all the assurance you really need. I'm home nights, I enjoy your company, I'm responsible. Isn't that love?

Discussion and Analysis

The change in behavior of one marital partner is always significant and can be traumatic. This is especially true if the change happens suddenly. Justifiably the mate must become suspicious. This apprehension will overshadow all other matters in the marriage and keep on snowballing until resolved. Certainly after many years of marriage the words "I love you" can hardly be expected to be repeated as often as before. Yet other signs of love must replace the phrase, such as small affections, services, and attentions. If they cease abruptly, then cause for concern develops.

One more word about love declarations. They are important particularly when husband and wife are temporarily apart, such as on vacations or business trips. A short, "I love you and miss you," over the phone or on a card will do wonders to a worried mate. Always though, when you feel unhappy about your companion, air the complaint. Nothing is worse than silent suffering, unless it is pouting.

THE MEMO METHOD APPLIED TO PROBLEMS OF THE FAMILY

PLAINTIFF: The Wife Who Felt Let Down

PROBLEM: I hate to tell you this, but your cousin Joe ogles me sometimes with impertinence. I feel uncomfortable in his presence. Let's avoid him.

Cause: He takes liberties because he knows you won't say anything, because you don't want to offend members of your family.

SOLUTION: Stop pleasing your family. They won't disown you if you stand up to them once in a while. In fact, they will respect you for it, and that goes for your cousin Joe, in particular.

REPLY

PROBLEM: You are always blaming me for trouble you get yourself into.

Cause: You seem to need the attention and flattery of men. When they take you up on your teasing, you pretend to be insulted.

SOLUTION: Pay more attention to me and not others. It is only important how we get along with each other.

Discussion and Analysis

Here again the Memo Method shows quite clearly how far apart these two persons are in each one understanding the other's problems. If the wife is correct, she will have a long way to go in convincing her defensive husband that he is weak and needs to learn how to develop a backbone. She may have hit upon a very serious problem if she is correct.

But the converse is also true. If the husband is right and it is true that his wife is a sexual tease, then she has a big problem and will have to change her behavior.

One can only speculate what the consequent discussion must have been like, because there is such little agreement over what the basic flaw in the family is. If the problem is essentially the wife's, then she will have to learn that being approved of is not all that important.

She is a worthwhile person whether she has the love and attention of other people or not.

If the problem is essentially the husband's, then he will have to learn that he too does not need the approval of his family and that giving in to them is not likely to get that approval. His wife would be quite correct to insist that he could get their respect more easily by not caring whether he had it. Only by showing them that he is an independent and strong person who is able to do without their approval will they regard him as a person worth knowing and respecting. If it is true that he gives in repeatedly, he is earning nothing but the disgust of those who might in fact now be insulting him further by making passes at his wife.

They have at least communicated. The difference in outlook is clearly shown by these two messages. They may have to take them to a marriage counselor before they can get them resolved.

PLAINTIFF: The Husband with the Rejected Mother

PROBLEM: You insist on inviting your parents every other Sunday, but when my mother visits once in a while you pretend important business and stay out. Why?

Cause 1: Her accent and simpleness seem to irritate you. You have not really talked to her in depth; therefore, you don't know how wise she can be.

SOLUTION 1: Force yourself to get to know her by taking her to lunch at times. Separate her background and lack of education from her and you won't be so prejudiced.

Cause 2: She's getting older, so sometimes she repeats herself and forgets what she's been talking about.

SOLUTION 2: If you wouldn't *let* those minor irritations get to you, your mood would quickly change to one of acceptance. It is not her behavior that upsets you, it's *your* thinking *about* her behavior that riles you up.

REPLY

PROBLEM: When your mother comes visiting, you often leave her with me to amuse her. It has only been lately (as I've told you before) that I've decided to force you to take your share of the responsibility by simply leaving the two of you together.

Cause 1: You get so wrapped up with your projects you forget that she's here for your company too.

SOLUTION 1: You practice what you've been thinking. If you keep pushing your mother off on me, there's got to be a reason. Figure it out!

Cause 2: You're right about my being irritated with some of her ways. We come from such different backgrounds.

SOLUTION 2: I'll have to make more of an effort to socialize with her, but only if you do your share too.

Discussion and Analysis

The tables were turned when the wife asked her husband to practice his own advice. If he can agree with her simple suggestion, their problem should ease off. Notable in this case is the sureness the wife showed in both standing up to his accusations and recognizing when he had a point to make.

Both partners have also wisely understood the basic psychological truth about who upsets whom. Each is responsible for his or her own disturbances, and they will not permit themselves to be falsely accused of behavior they are incapable of. They know that the older woman's behavior was not really the main issue at all. It was their conflict over each other that was brought into focus by the Memo Method. Even though much of that written conversation had been gone over several times in the form of quarrels, this time, with leisure to study each other's thoughts as a memo, they understood each other.

PLAINTIFF: The Wife Who Was Afraid to Upset Her Husband

PROBLEM: I often want to talk to you about touchy matters, but you react so strongly I have learned to say nothing that upsets you. How can I approach you?

Cause 1: Am I in your opinion not intelligent enough to make a good conversational partner? I know I am just a housewife and in comparison to you not educated, but I have done a lot of reading and can match you in many fields.

SOLUTION 1: Suggest subjects and give me the material. I shall gladly beef up on them to give you a good challenge.

Cause 2: I guess you are tired after work and would rather read or just talk small talk. I, on the other hand, yearn for some intellectual arguments after a day in the kitchen.

SOLUTION 2: I'll let you rest for a whole hour after dinner, but then you'll have no excuse to act tired. Besides, I want to cheer you up when something goes wrong at work. "Shared trouble is half the trouble," as they say.

Cause 3: Are you afraid a talk may unveil touchy subjects you would like to avoid? Why? It is inconsiderate of you to cut me short.

SOLUTION 3: I can take anything better than silence. If there is someone you share your interests with better, I must know. We shall either overcome this problem or try to find another solution, even separation.

REPLY

PROBLEM: Lately you have been finding fault with me about everything. I have not changed.

Cause: I guess it is you who are tense and may be bored from sitting at home all day long.

SOLUTION: Why don't you find an occupation? You will better understand the pleasure of silence after working in loud surroundings.

Discussion and Analysis

The argument gets heated, and more than ever the Memo Method is essential in bringing out the facts. The husband has countered by a complaint of his own and he may be right. It could be that the nervousness of the wife, who had been doing only housework but has really greater ambitions, is the cause of the problem. Though husband and wife will exchange ideas and experiences, they need the stimulation of outsiders also.

It is not easy to admit sensitive shortcomings such as intelligence or sophistication. These matters can often be dealt with more easily when put in writing.

Again we see how one problem usually creates others. Not being fulfilled in one area of her life, the wife imagined neglect with respect to her husband. These types of problems are very sensitive and can hurt deeply if not understood. When you can't talk about them, try writing about them.

THE MEMO METHOD APPLIED TO PROBLEMS OF SEX

PLAINTIFF: A Frustrated Husband

PROBLEM: Sometimes, although I want you, I wait for you to start, and when you do not I am frustrated and hurt.

Cause 1: You think you have to play the passive role.

SOLUTION 1: You'd still be feminine even if aggressive. Society and stale moral codes have changed—and what's more, I'll love it.

Cause 2: We have a habit going. You expect me to make all the advances because that's what we've always done.

SOLUTION 2: After I've made an overture I will not

make another until you reciprocate. This will force you to be less impassive.

REPLY

> PROBLEM: I *do* make overtures, but you don't notice them.

Cause 1: My advances are more subtle than yours.

> SOLUTION 1: Consider it as a general rule that if I snuggle up to you in the bedroom I am ready.

Cause 2: I don't want to play games. Responding to you each time after you have responded to me makes our relationship too mechanical.

> SOLUTION 2: Let me make my advances in my own way and at my own speed. Even then, I don't think I can be aggressive. I just wasn't raised that way.

Discussion and Analysis

It is apparent that this couple will have to have serious discussions and perhaps write other memos. They have not resolved their difficulties by any means, nor have they agreed as to the major cause of their problems. The husband is right; in this day and age he may expect his wife to make approximately as many sexual advances as he does. There is no logical reason why he should be the initiator, although this has been our belief in society for hundreds of years.

The wife is wrong to suppose that passivity makes her more feminine and she must not push. It is not a woman's nature just to be seduced; that is a matter of training. Just as she learns to be a passive recipient of love, she can also learn to be an aggressive go-getter for love. If this is what makes her husband happy, then why should he not expect her to do what she expects of him?

In all likelihood this impasse in the marriage will resolve itself when the wife learns to be less subtle, when she becomes more blatant in her techniques of showing that she wants to have sex.

If she does not respond with additional overtures of lovemaking when he has made them before and waits for her to respond, then serious trouble might enter the marriage. This could simply bring things to a head. Once having surfaced, the fundamental issues involved here can be dealt with again until some satisfactory compromise is reached. But it is anticipated that things are bound to get worse before they get better.

THE MEMO METHOD APPLIED TO PROBLEMS OF VACATIONS

PLAINTIFF: A Man Who Made Too Many Decisions

PROBLEM: I always have to decide our vacation plans, but afterward I get criticized by the whole family if something goes wrong.

Cause 1: No one wants to take the risk of making a bad decision.

SOLUTION 1: Next year I refuse to make any plans as to where we go. You and the kids decide and I'll follow.

Cause 2: You are afraid of making mistakes, so you shy

away from them and let me stick my neck out. You think you're worthless if you make mistakes.

SOLUTION 2: Get some counseling to show you how to accept yourself even if your reasoning is imperfect.

REPLY

PROBLEM: I had no idea you felt this way. I don't believe I shy away from making decisions for the reasons you stated. I thought all along you resented my suggestions, so I've learned to keep quiet.

Cause: You get so mad when I don't agree with you completely that I'd rather say nothing than get into a fight.

SOLUTION: From now on I'll talk up more even if we quarrel. If we disagree civilly, we should find out what each of us really feels.

Discussion and Analysis

The difficulty in this marriage is a fairly typical one. One person believes one set of conditions prevails, while the other person has no inkling of this at all and believes an entirely different set of conditions prevails. The husband in this case thinks his wife does not want to make suggestions, while the wife feels that the husband does not want her to make suggestions. This is precisely why a memo such as this is valuable. It frequently brings these inconsistencies to light.

The husband's first solution, that he will not make suggestions the coming year, is an excellent one because it will force the family to handle the situation if they truly are afraid to risk making judgments. It is hoped, however, they would begin to see their respective roles somewhat differently and get over this initial period of needing to prove something to each other.

The second solution, that his wife get counseling, would make sense in this case only if it is true that she is afraid of making decisions. According to her, this is not the case, and therefore this solution would not apply. However, experience will tell whether he is right or wrong.

The wife's solution, that they perhaps have more quarrels, is also a healthy one, since it will at least force communication rather than silence where important facts such as the above cannot be communicated. There may be a few more stormy scenes in the house, but if important messages are getting communicated, this will be worth the momentary unpleasantness that might result.

THE MEMO METHOD APPLIED TO PROBLEMS OF CHILDREN

PLAINTIFF: A Mother Who Is Concerned About Her Son

PROBLEM: Your son waited all day long to talk and play with you. Give him some attention even if it is for a short time only. The newspaper and the television can wait. He feels rejected.

Cause 1: Why did you always say you wanted a son if you do not have patience with children?

SOLUTION 1: Could it be that you have a problem in relating to your son? Can I help?

Cause 2: You are tired from a hard day of work and have not read the latest news. I can understand, but how shall I explain all this to your son?

SOLUTION 2: Try to interest your son in the television show you prefer and read him some items from the paper. That way everyone will be happy.

Cause 3: Junior is rambunctious and fidgety. Does he make you nervous?

SOLUTION 3: Do you think there is something wrong with the boy? Is he overactive? I cannot see it. Being with him all day somewhat distorts my view and objectivity. Shall we see a child psychologist?

REPLY

I am all keyed up after a hectic day. Reading the paper or watching television unwinds me. He will just have to learn to wait until I am ready to talk to him.

Discussion and Analysis

How can an overly tired man just home from a busy day at the office step into his role as father of an active son? He desires to have a drink and read the paper first, but the boy wants attention. It is a difficult decision, but it has to be made. Of course playing with the child should be not a duty but a pleasure. Also, as the wife suggested, the son could partially participate in watching the show and even share news items in the paper, a good way to educate him. If a father shirks the education of a child, he need not complain later if the child cuts his connection with the home quite early and becomes noncommunicative. A child needs both parents, and a half hour intensively spent is often enough to maintain the image of a loving, caring parent.

PLAINTIFF: A Mother Who Fears that Her Son Is Getting Spoiled

PROBLEM: The last time I refused our son's request for money I found out you had slipped him some. Do you think he will respect you for this?

Cause: I suspect you want to get into his good favor to spite me. I know you have been angry with me lately, and you know how much it bothers me to see you use our son against me.

SOLUTION: Come to me directly with your complaints rather than show your resentment by using the boy against me. Better still, don't get angry with me at all, but allow me the right as a human being to have views of my own that sometimes differ from yours.

REPLY

PROBLEM: As usual, you are making too much out of an innocent act. I do not give our son money to spite you. I give it to him because I just don't think that we have to be as hard on him as you are.

Cause: You were quite spoiled as a child, and I think you have a right to be concerned about spoiling him. However, in your zeal to protect him against being a brat you're being so severe that you punish him needlessly.

SOLUTION: Have some of that tolerance *for* me which you want to have *from* me. I too am human and do not always know that the boy might be manipulating me against you. I do not do it to get even with you. Let's both of us watch, that we are not misused.

Discussion and Analysis

This problem has to be talked over at considerable length before these parents can reach a harmonious conclusion. Each of them is still sure that he or she is right and until they both learn how to be less suspicious of the other they are certainly not going to have the marriage they might otherwise have. The suggestion made that they should not use the child as a weapon against either one is, of course, the most important observation brought out by this exchange of memos. Little else that happens aside from this is as important as that single issue. It goes without saying that further memos will have to be exchanged before the husband and wife reach a reasonable balance of power.

THE MEMO METHOD APPLIED TO FINANCES
PLAINTIFF: A Spouse Who Felt Cheated

PROBLEM: I notice most of our money goes for pleasure and clothes for you. Whenever I need something for the house, you claim budgetary difficulties. Let's make the arrangements fairer.

Cause 1: You are a spendthrift because, as a single child, your parents gave you everything. You get used to thinking of yourself first.

SOLUTION 1: Accept your new responsibilities as head of a family! And remember that each of us has to have a share of the income.

Cause 2: You think you have to show off before your friends at the country club and have drinks on you.

SOLUTION 2: Don't you see they just misuse your childish attitude of self-importance? They should respect you for yourself, not for the drinks you buy.

Cause 3: You are a health faddist and believe too much in the benefits of skiing, tennis, etc. You love your looks so much that you overspend to keep up physical appearances.

SOLUTION 3: Stop acting like an adolescent.

REPLY

You don't understand that clothes make people in my business. Because those guys at the country club are so gullible and impressed, I act like a big shot. The final financial gain is worth my initial spending. If you think the budget cannot cover these expenses, you should look for a job to help cover some of your less important needs.

Discussion and Analysis

This marriage suffers from noncommunication between husband and wife. He seems to think that only he is entitled to make money decisions. If it really was as he stated, he should have confided in his wife and told her why he was such a free spender. His suggestion to her to get a job is an insult and shows his egocentric standpoint. Unless they get together and do a lot of talking or writing of memos, the marriage is on the rocks.

PLAINTIFF: The Wife Who Was Shortchanged

PROBLEM: Let me open my own account. It makes me feel important and responsible.

Cause: You have very little confidence in me and think you have to take over everything. Sometimes I feel like your daughter instead of your wife.

SOLUTION: Let's cut the umbilical cord. I want to grow up. Perhaps I have not shown a desire to mature before, but I insist upon it now. Therefore, to be consistent I will simply take it upon myself as an adult to open an account of extra monies that I can earn through my part-time work and whatever I can spare from our budget.

REPLY

PROBLEM: I am delighted to see that you finally have the courage to take the bull by the horns and do what an adult is supposed to do. I haven't been against this as much as you think. When I protested, it was only to test you to see how much you would take before you had the courage to stand up for yourself.

SOLUTION: Do more of this kind of thing. You don't always have to have my approval for all your actions. Even if I disapprove, you have to live with that. If you want to have the responsibility and independence you claim, then you will have to face the frustrations that go along with it. One of these frustrations may be my disapproval from time to time, particularly of your failure to handle money matters wisely.

Discussion and Analysis

This couple is on the road to a very fine marriage. The husband in this case has an unusual grasp of the psychological principles for inducing growth. He knows that it cannot be handed over to someone, it must be earned. He is not babying his wife by letting her win anything easily. She must earn it the hard way, as all adults earn respect and gain experience—the hard way.

He is also quite correct in anticipating where she may weaken. All her suggestions will not fall on receptive ears. If she can learn to stick to her guns and tolerate his momentary disapproval, she will succeed in achieving full recognition and respect.

THE MEMO METHOD APPLIED TO RELIGION

PLAINTIFF: A Parent Who Is Concerned Over the Children's Religious Education

PROBLEM: We had decided not to follow any particular religious tradition. Now you have started decorating the house for the holidays and are insisting upon the children going to your place of worship.

Cause 1: Your family is putting pressure on you to raise the children in their faith.

SOLUTION 1: I strongly advise that we follow our neutral course as we agreed upon when we were married. Perhaps we could talk to your family's minister, who may support us in this dispute. He is fair enough to see that a forced solution may destroy our marriage.

Cause 2: I think your tendency to allow your parents to manipulate you has grown again since you have become ill and have had to lean upon them. Your mother has helped you out, and I think you are feeling guilty and therefore are trying to please her by making this concession to her.

SOLUTION 2: Perhaps we should move away so that she has less hold over you. Or perhaps I could talk to her and simply take a firm stand. After all, I don't owe her any loyalty.

REPLY

PROBLEM: I think you are right. I am dominated by my mother again since I have let her do so much for me. I was simply hoping that you would not mind if we went back to my faith. Now that I know that it does bother you I feel I want to agree with you and do what you feel is best in the situation.

Discussion and Analysis

We see here that it is not necessary for the wife to come out with causes and solutions to a problem she understands. Her husband has been perceptive in this instance and has hit the nail on the head. Why delve into an issue more than is called for when it is apparent that agreement is near at hand? She is wise not to raise other issues and to let the matter rest as it is. No doubt their former harmony will prevail if she continues to offer little resistance in this sensitive matter of religion and stick without reservation to the premarital agreement between her and her husband.

Postscript

GO TO IT

In the preceding pages you have been given some of the fundamentals for a sound and happy marriage. They may seem deceptively simple, but they are not easy to implement. It takes much work to face frustrations, to grow up to be patient and tolerant adults, and to put the welfare of the marriage above your own personal preferences of the moment. Remember, you cannot be happy in a marriage unless the other person is happy also. It is impossible for a marriage to succeed while one person is happy and the other person is miserable. To make your marriage work, therefore, you want to make sure that you are reasonably happy but that your mate also is reasonably happy.

No one gets his or her way all the time. The couples that allow one mate to become consistently satisfied while the other mate is consistently frustrated are not going to have a marriage for very long. Therefore, the very next time you come up against frustrations and you find that your mate is not listening to you, swing into action. Do something so that what you are saying can be seen through the eyes rather than just heard through the ears.

Another way to get your message through is to write

it down on paper and have it read just as you are reading our thoughts on paper. The technique that we espouse in this book will work. We have both had experience to indicate that this is so. Our additional remarks have been intended to strengthen your resolve to stand up for yourself, to take reasonable positions, and to be able to discuss where you have a right to protest and when you do not. When you feel you do have that right, then by all means jot down your complaint, analyze its cause, and offer the best proposals to solve it that you can think of.

Keep copies of your memos. You will want to review these remarks occasionally and to study the history of your marriage as it relates to the frustrations you have had. Imagine looking back over this record twenty years from now and noticing what your complaints were way back then and how far you have come because the two of you had open communication.

PROBLEM

Cause

SOLUTION

PROBLEM

Cause

SOLUTION

PROBLEM

Cause

SOLUTION

Recommended Reading

Ellis, Albert, and Harper, Robert, *Creative Marriage.* Lyle Stuart, Inc., 1961. Reprinted as *A Guide to Successful Marriage.* Wilshire Book Co., 1972.

The sound principles of rational-emotive therapy (RET) are applied to the specific conditions of marriage. Ellis and Harper are experienced psychologists and marriage counselors. This is one of the few books on marriage using the RET method. Learning to stand up for oneself while being reasonably calm is one of the aims of this work.

Ellis, Albert, *The Art and Science of Love.* Lyle Stuart, Inc., 1960. Reprint. Bantam Books, Inc., 1969.

This paperback is regarded as one of the best sex manuals on the market. It reads easily, it is practical, and it instructs the reader in correcting sexual problems through rational-emotive therapy.

Hauck, Paul, *The Rational Management of Children,* 2d rev. ed. Libra Publishers, Inc., 1972.

Differences in disciplining children, assigning them responsibilities, and understanding their annoying behaviors can be among the most vexing problems in a marriage. The RET method is applied in this book to the numerous misbehaviors of children, and the parent is advised through instruction and example how to cope with disturbed children.

Hauck, Paul A., *Overcoming Depression*. The Westminster Press, 1973.

For those who feel unequal in their marriages, who are ridden with guilt and frequently depressed, who are bound to have problems in relationships with their mates. This paperback instructs in nonprofessional language how to combat psychological depression and to overcome guilt. Getting rid of these disturbances has to make a mate stronger in standing up for his or her rights in marriage.

Hauck, Paul A., *Overcoming Frustration and Anger*. The Westminster Press, 1974.

Another easy-to-read paperback, this time geared to help control the most destructive emotion to marriage. Few relationships can survive constant hostility, faultfinding, nagging, and resentment. Unless anger is kept within reasonable bounds, a marriage will simply not be all it might be. In simple language this book can teach the emotional control needed to make a marriage succeed.

Lederer, William J., and Jackson, Don D., *The Mirages of Marriage*. W. W. Norton & Company, Inc., 1968.

This book provides many interesting insights into what marriage is really all about. Of special interest are the types of marriages people arrange, the destructive elements in marriages, and the need to establish a *bargaining* practice to reach harmony between the mates.